STEPHEN KING
THE STAND
Hardcases

THE STAND: HARDCASES. Contains material originally published in magazine form as THE STAND: HARDCASES #1-5. First printing 2011. ISBN# 978-0-7851-3623-1. Published by MARVEL WORLDWIDE, INC., a subsidiary of MARVEL ENTERTAINMENT, LLC. OFFICE OF PUBLICATION: 135 West 50th Street, New York, NY 10020. Copyright © 2010 and 2011 Stephen King. All rights reserved. $24.99 per copy in the U.S. and $27.99 in Canada (GST #R127032852); Canadian Agreement #40668537. All characters featured in this publication and the distinctive names and likenesses thereof, and all related indicia are trademarks of Stephen King. Published by arrangement with The Doubleday Broadway Publishing Group, a division of Random House, Inc. This publication is produced under license from The Doubleday Broadway Publishing Group and Stephen King. No similarity between any of the names, characters, persons, and/or institutions in this book with those of any living or dead person or institution is intended, and any such similarity which may exist is purely coincidental. Marvel and its logos are TM & © Marvel Characters, Inc. **Printed in the U.S.A.** ALAN FINE, EVP - Office of the President, Marvel Worldwide, Inc. and EVP & CMO Marvel Characters B.V.; DAN BUCKLEY, Chief Executive Officer and Publisher - Print, Animation & Digital Media; JIM SOKOLOWSKI, Chief Operating Officer; DAVID GABRIEL, SVP of Publishing Sales & Circulation; DAVID BOGART, SVP of Business Affairs & Talent Management; MICHAEL PASCIULLO, VP Merchandising & Communications; JIM O'KEEFE, VP of Operations & Logistics; DAN CARR, Executive Director of Publishing Technology; JUSTIN F. GABRIE, Director of Publishing & Editorial Operations; SUSAN CRESPI, Editorial Operations Manager; ALEX MORALES, Publishing Operations Manager; STAN LEE, Chairman Emeritus. For information regarding advertising in Marvel Comics or on Marvel.com, please contact Ron Stern, VP of Business Development, at rstern@marvel.com. For Marvel subscription inquiries, please call 800-217-9158. **Manufactured between 1/3/2011 and 1/31/2011 by R.R. DONNELLEY, INC., SALEM, VA, USA.**

10 9 8 7 6 5 4 3 2 1

STEPHEN KING

THE STAND

HARDCASES

Creative Director and Executive Director
STEPHEN KING

Script
ROBERTO AGUIRRE-SACASA

Art
MIKE PERKINS

Color Art
LAURA MARTIN

Lettering
VC'S RUS WOOTON

Production
IRENE Y. LEE & DAN REMOLLINO

Assistant Editor
CHARLIE BECKERMAN

Consulting Editors
MICHAEL HORWITZ & BILL ROSEMANN

Senior Editor
RALPH MACCHIO

Cover Art
TOMM COKER WITH LAURA MARTIN

Collection Editor
MARK D. BEAZLEY

Editorial Assistants
JOE HOCHSTEIN & JAMES EMMETT

Assistant Editors:
NELSON RIBEIRO & ALEX STARBUCK

Editor, Special Projects
JENNIFER GRUNWALD

Senior Editor, Special Projects
JEFF YOUNGQUIST

Senior Vice President of Publishing Sales
DAVID GABRIEL

Senior Vice President of Strategic Development
RUWAN JAYATILLEKE

Book Designer
SPRING HOTELING

Editor in Chief
JOE QUESADA

Publisher
DAN BUCKLEY

Special Thanks to Chuck Verrill, Marsha DeFilippo, , Brian Stark,
Jim Nausedas, Jim McCann, Arune Singh, Lauren Sankovitch, & Jeff Suter

For more information on THE STAND comics, visit marvel.com/comics/the_stand

To find Marvel Comics at a local comic shop, call 1-888-COMICBOOK

INTRODUCTION

...BY THE PEOPLE

Hardcases is a crucial volume in the progression of THE STAND. Up until now, it's all been about survival—just staying alive. It's been quite a harrowing journey for our intrepid protagonists. They've fled corpse-filled cities and overcome tremendous obstacles on the road. Now, things have stabilized a bit out in Boulder, Colorado, where the group has gathered. Something monumental in scope is about to take place.

Man is an organizational animal, to a greater extent than any other primate. And here, a little farther west than the heartland of the country, no less than the recreation of the United States of America is undertaken! I remember when I first read THE STAND how that thought hit me like a bolt of lightning. Stephen King was taking his narrative to a place I never suspected. It was fascinating to read all the character interactions—particularly the bizarre triangle involving Stu, Frannie and Howard, and the shared trip undertaken by the Trashcan Man and The Kid. But this nation building idea I didn't see coming.

There's a scene at the opening of issue three of this story arc which is pivotal. Yet, it's quiet and serene in presentation. Just two men sitting on a park bench discussing the United States, phase two. Just two fine fellows having a chat, making plans to recreate the government of the United States, beginning with the ratification of the Declaration of Independence, the Constitution and the Bill of Rights. And the next step is to run the government as if it were a New England township; a perfect democracy. I was struck by what an audacious and yet perfectly logical outgrowth of the survival process this was. If Man can claw his way back from the brink, and stick around long enough, he is going to form a society. It's inevitable. And it made me reflect on the fragile nature of our Republic, robust though it appears to be.

And in the reality of THE STAND, all parties concerned plan to formulate the new government around one person as its titular head—the blessed Mother Abigail. But the caveat is that this very old, very independent woman has her own ideas about it all. And suddenly, things may not go according to the master plan. That's the beauty of THE STAND, and that's life. Enjoy

Ralph Macchio
December, 2010

PREVIOUSLY

Two months ago, something happened at Project Blue in California. Within weeks, a flu-like virus—"Captain Trips"—swept through the world, killing 99% of the population. Now, it's up to the survivors to piece together a new life in a world that has moved on.

Three rag-tag groups have started to pick their way West. Nick Andros, a deaf-mute who lost an eye during the last gasping throes of Captain Trips, has met up with Abagail Freemantle, a 108-year-old woman in Nebraska. With him are Ralph Brentner, Dick Ellis, and the man-child Tom Cullen, with half a dozen others, and all together, they are heading to Colorado.

Frannie Goldsmith and Harold Lauder have connected with Glen Bateman and Stu Redman, and they too are making their way to Nebraska to meet up with the woman they've come to know in their dreams as Mother Abagail. However, tension is brewing in the group, as Stu and Frannie have struck up a romance, much to the chagrin of Harold...

Larry Underwood traveled alone for a while, until he met up with Nadine Cross and a boy, Joe, who doesn't speak. They have met others, and they are following a dream of an old woman in a shack in Nebraska. It is a dream they all share... all of them, except Nadine.

There is another force drawing the survivors to him, to Las Vegas, and he goes by many names: the Dark Man, Randall Flagg, the Hardcase. No one knows where he came from, but everyone—even his allies—fear him. The pieces are being moved into place...but to what end, no one knows.

chapter ONE

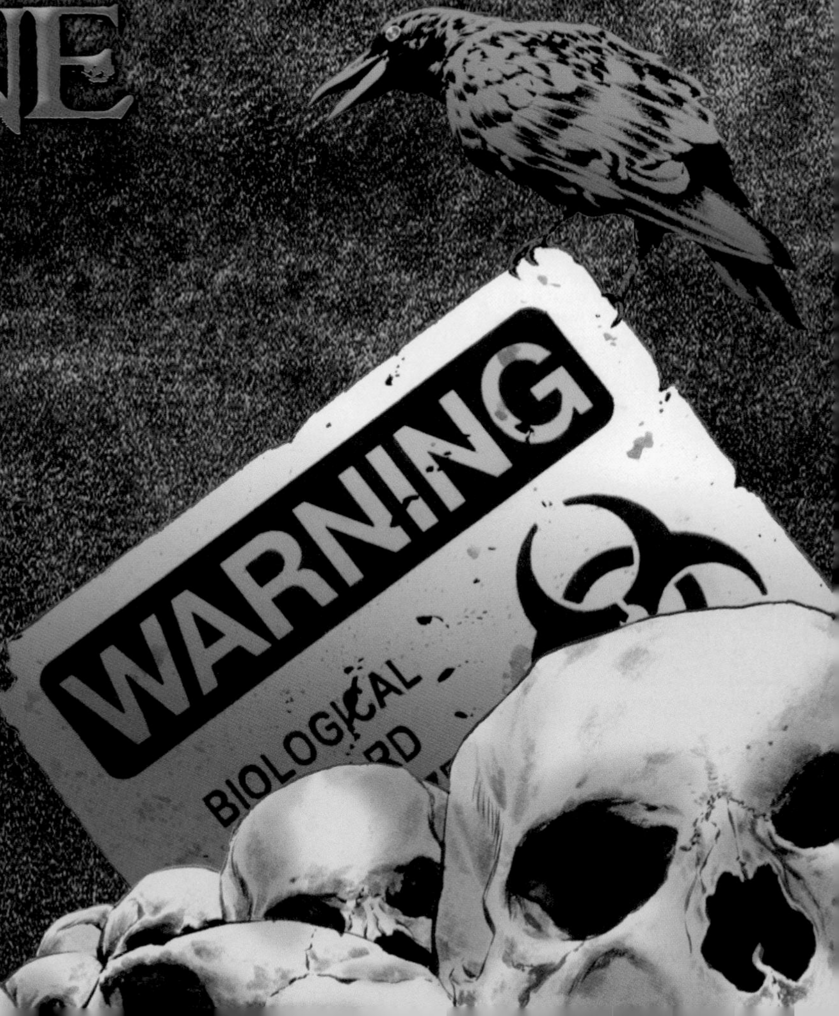
WARNING
BIOLOGICAL

MEANWHILE. INTERSTATE 15.

The man who was once Donald Merwin Elbert, now Trashcan Man forever and ever, beheld the fabled City, Seven in One...

Cibola. The City that is Promised. The City of Dreams.

I'm coming... I'll do whatever you want...

My life for you...

His body a broken, burnt wreck, as mad as a hatter from walking through God's frying pan with no rest and no water, Trashy began to dance.

Ci-a-bola, Ci-a-bola, bump-ty, bump-ty *bump!*

Ci-a-bola, Ci-a-bola, bump-ty, bump-ty *bump!*

Tonight, he thought, he would drink from the waters of Cibola, and they would taste like wine.

And then he would find *him*, the man who had bade him across the plains and mountains and, finally, into the desert.

He who Is--the Dark Man, the hardcase.

His were the armies of the night, his were the white-faced riders of the dead...

Soon, there would be things Trashcan cared for very little:

Shrieks and rapes, subjugation and murder--

I will set you high in my artillery. You are the man I want.

--but, also very soon, there would be a Great Burning.
And about *that*, Trashcan Man cared very much.

Cibola...

A MONTH EARLIER.

The first dream had come to Trashcan Man in Gary, Indiana, after a mishap blowing up the town's oil tanks left him unconscious.

There had been a blinding white flare--

Then agony, as though he'd thrust his arm into an active volcano, churning lava--

He made it off the tank in one piece, barely, falling part of the way and landing on his arm, smothering the flames.

As he lost consciousness, he murmured:

Live by the torch, die...

...by...

...the...

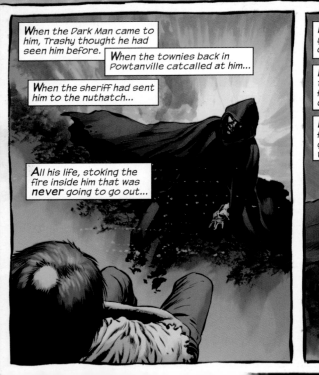

When the Dark Man came to him, Trashy thought he had seen him before.

When the townies back in Powtanville catcalled at him...

When the sheriff had sent him to the nuthatch...

All his life, stoking the fire inside him that was **never** going to go out...

His was the face you could never quite see...

His were the hands that dealt spades from the death deck...

His was the grin from beyond the grave of the world...

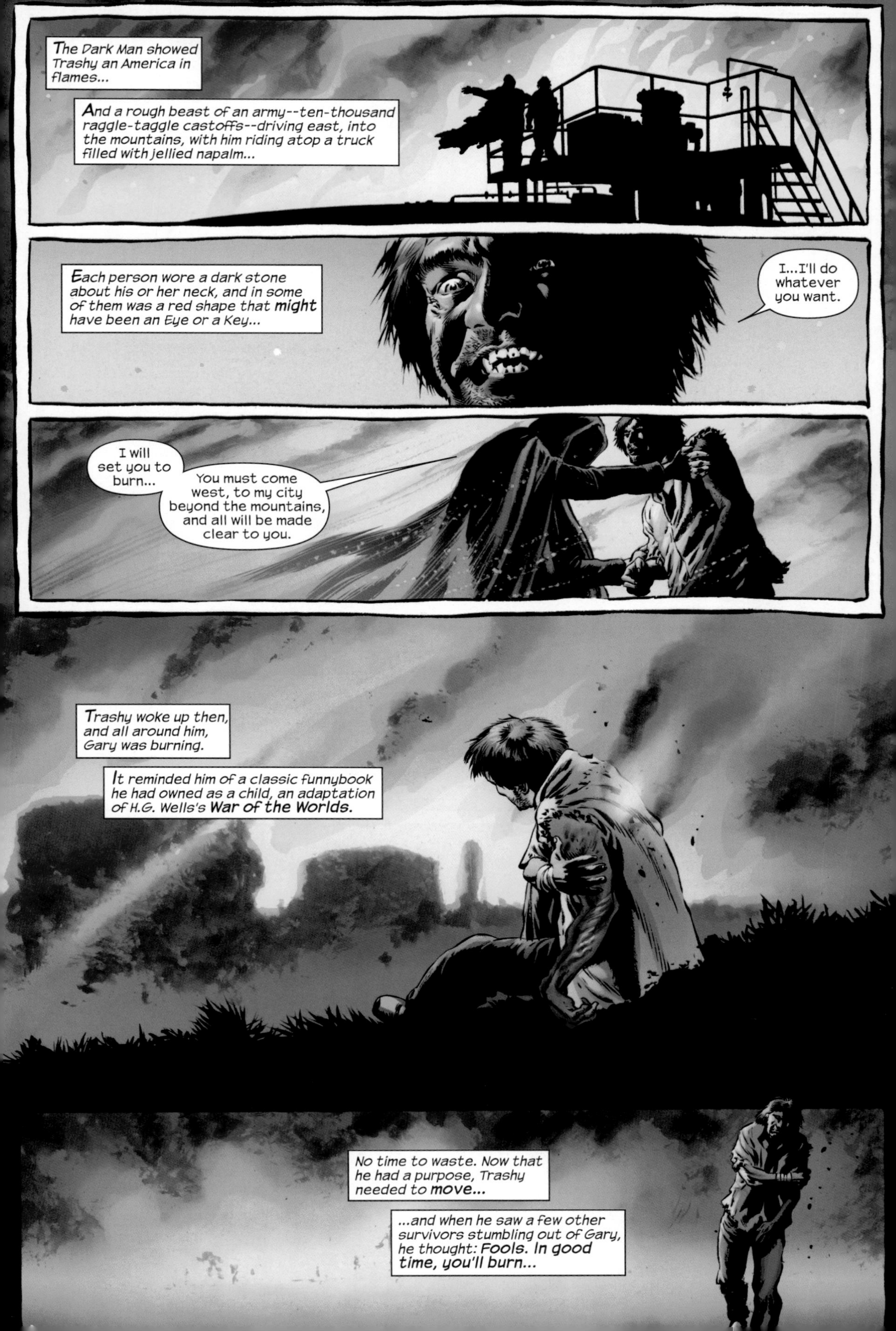
The Dark Man showed Trashy an America in flames...
And a rough beast of an army--ten-thousand raggle-taggle castoffs--driving east, into the mountains, with him riding atop a truck filled with jellied napalm...
Each person wore a dark stone about his or her neck, and in some of them was a red shape that might have been an Eye or a Key...
I...I'll do whatever you want.
I will set you to burn...
You must come west, to my city beyond the mountains, and all will be made clear to you.
Trashy woke up then, and all around him, Gary was burning.
It reminded him of a classic funnybook he had owned as a child, an adaptation of H.G. Wells's War of the Worlds.
No time to waste. Now that he had a purpose, Trashy needed to move...
...and when he saw a few other survivors stumbling out of Gary, he thought: Fools. In good time, you'll burn...

On July 4th, the day Larry Underwood discovered Rita Blakemoor had overdosed, Trashcan Man began riding a ten-speed.

He fell off *twice* that first day, once squarely on his burn, which he slathered in Vaseline and antiseptic to ward off gangrene.

On July 8th, the day Nick and Tom saw buffalo grazing in Comanche County, Trashcan Man crossed the Mississippi into Iowa.

On the fourteenth, he crossed the Missouri...

...and, for the first time since Gary, Trash suspected that God Himself might intervene between him and his destiny.

He was in Nebraska, and there was something dreadfully wrong...

In Nebraska, at night, the Dark Man-- his constant companion since Indiana--came to him no more.

Instead, he began to dream about...

...an old woman?

Singing songs Trashy vaguely knew.

Songs the mother of a boy named Donald Merwin Elbert used to sing while doing her housework.

He'd be peering at her, paralyzed with hate and fear, because all of a sudden, the woman would stop her singing and--

Weasel in the corn!

And he would look down to see--

And then he would scream himself awake--

Oh please det

Which is how Trashcan Man ended up crossing four hundred miles in three days, running mostly on high octane terror.

(For Mother Abagail's part, she awoke during the night of July 15-- just as Trashcan Man passed north of Hemmingford Home-- full of fear and pity.)

(She thought she might have been dreaming about her grandson Andres, who'd been killed in a hunting accident when he was six.)

On July 18, southwest of Sterling, Colorado, a '32 Ford deuce coupe screeched to a halt right next to Trashy on Highway 34.

It, and its driver, were a sight to behold.

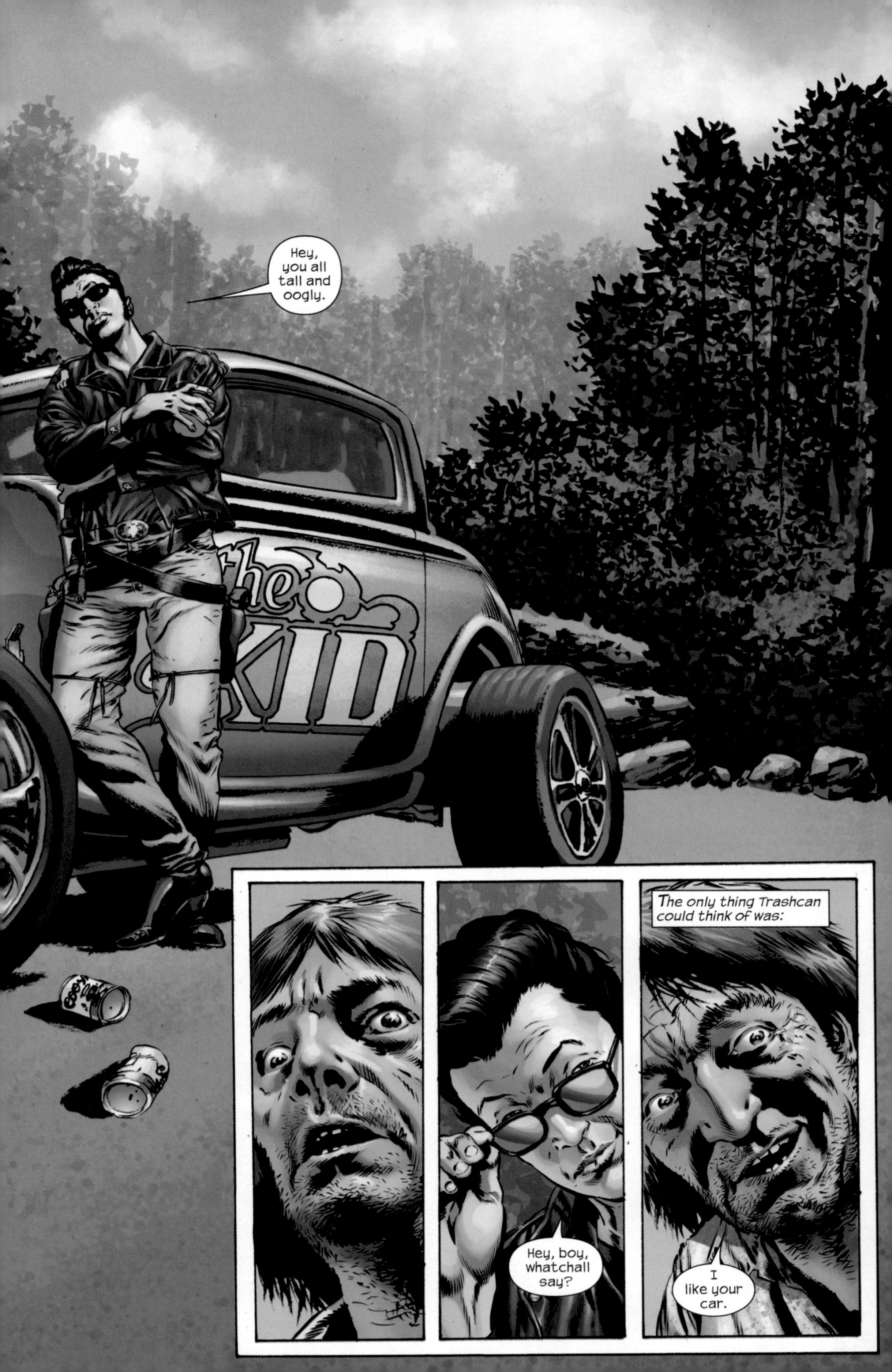
Hey, you all tall and oogly.
the KID
The only thing Trashcan could think of was:
Hey, boy, whatchall say?
I like your car.

It was, perhaps, the *only* right thing to say.

Five minutes later, Trashy was riding shotgun as the deuce coupe accelerated to the Kid's cruising speed, 95 MPH.

They call me the Kid. Outta Shreeport Looseyanna. This here beast won every major carshow award in the South. You believe that happy crappy...?

What they call you, boy?

The Trashcan Man.

Because I used to light fires in people's trashcans and mailboxes and stuff.

Didja? Boy, you sound crazy, but that's all right. I like crazy people.

I'm crazy myself.

Almost as if to prove the point, they whizzed around a bend and just missed slamming into a overturned Belkins semi--

Skimmed by the cab of the truck with a coat of paint to spare--

The Kid never turned a hair.

No sense beatin' around the bush. I guess we're going to the same place. I guess you been getting dreams about that boogeyman in the black flight-suit, am I right?

You mean the priest? Yeah...

Spooky, ain't he?

But he don't scare me. He's a hard baby, but the Kid's handled hard babies before. I shut 'em up, then shut 'em down--

You know what I'm gonna do after we get west?

I'm gonna lay low for a while. Check out the situation. Check out the big man, happy crappy. And then...

Then... what?

Gonna shut him down. Send him around dead man's curve. Put him out to pasture and take over.

You stick with me, Trashman, or whatever you call yerself...

...and we're gonna eat more chicken than any man ever seen.

Trash and the Kid checked into adjoining rooms in a motel in Golden, Colorado.

BLAMMM!!!

The Kid, drunk on warm Coors, was in a mood...

No 'lectricity, no TV, don't I *hate* that... I *love* it that all the shitheads got wasted, but where's my HBO? Where's my Playboy Channel? Where's...?

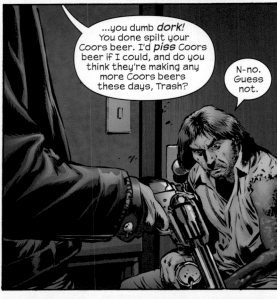

...you dumb *dork!* You done spilt your Coors beer. I'd *piss* Coors beer if I could, and do you think they're making any more Coors beers these days, Trash?

N-no. Guess not.

You're damn right, it's a dangered *spee-shees.*

I'm gonna ventilate your thinking-machine for being so wasteful, you believe that happy crappy?

Trashcan Man did. He thought it was the end of his life, for sure.

I'll tell you what, Trash. You get you another can of Coors, and you *chug* it. If you can chug the whole thing, I won't send you to the Cadillac Ranch.

Go on. Every drop. And if you puke it back up, you're a gone goose.

-FFSSHHTT-

Warm beer gurgled out, into Trashy's throat.

He swallowed convulsively.

And swallowed.

And swallowed.

When the can was empty, and after a seemingly endless battle with his gorge, Trashy won his life back in one long--

BURP

Ah-hah HA!

Okay, not bad, Trashcan Man. Not too damn shabby...

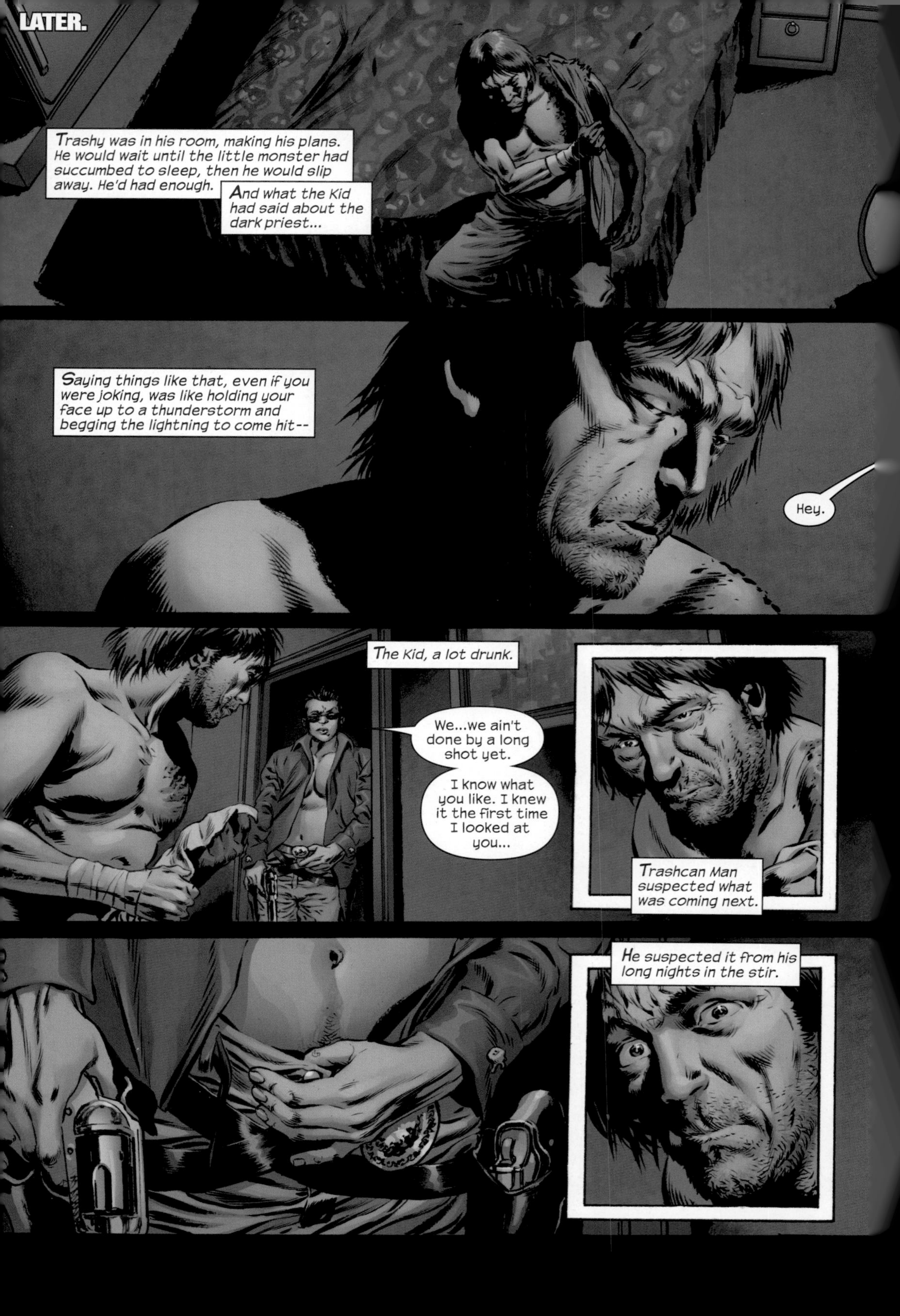

LATER.
Trashy was in his room, making his plans. He would wait until the little monster had succumbed to sleep, then he would slip away. He'd had enough.
And what the Kid had said about the dark priest...
Saying things like that, even if you were joking, was like holding your face up to a thunderstorm and begging the lightning to come hit--
Hey.
The Kid, a lot drunk.
We...we ain't done by a long shot yet.
I know what you like. I knew it the first time I looked at you...
Trashcan Man suspected what was coming next.
He suspected it from his long nights in the stir.

Mercifully, after it was over-- after the Kid had finished his business--sleep came.

And with sleep, a dream...

He was on a dark road, and very high.

Don't worry, I will give you a sign...

I will show you what happens to those who would set themselves against me.

Wait and watch, my good and faithful servant...

Hey, pusbag, wake up. We got us a big day ahead. Lotta stuff gonna happen today, am I right?

My life for yours...

S-sure hope you are.

INTERSTATE 70.
DUSK, AFTER A DAY OF SLOW DRIVING.

I don't believe it... I don't...effin'... B'LEEVE IT!

GET OUTTA MY ROAD! YOU'RE ALL DEAD! Y'ALL BELONG IN THE BONEYARD, YOU GOT NO BUSINESS ON MY EFFIN' ROAD!

Colorado Rocky Mountain high, *Trashcan Man thought, I've seen it raining Chevies in the sky...* And then he giggled.

That's it, I'm gonna kill you, Trashy--I'm gonna take your life--but first...

....first, you're gonna clear this mess for me.

C-clear...?

All of...?

I'm not leaving my car, no way, no how.

Now you get pushing, Trashy, and you push fast enough, maybe I **won't** blow your brains out, you believe that happy crappy?

Trashy offered a silent prayer up to the Dark Man...

Come on, ya wet end dummy, getcha back in it...

Pain flared in Trashy's recently burned arm; he knew that the fragile new tissue would soon rip...

The pain would become agony.

An impossible task. The Kid would get bored soon, and then...

What the hell was that?

I didn't hear anyth--

Who's there? You better answer me or I start shooting!

The Kid was answered, but not by a human voice.

By a howl that rose up like a hoarse siren, first climbing then dropping into a guttural growl.

They were coming down the slope on the far side of the turnpike and crossing the median.

The Kid emptied his .45s, but only dropped three wolves. Three...of two dozen? More?

BLAMM!!
BLAMM!!
BLAMM!!

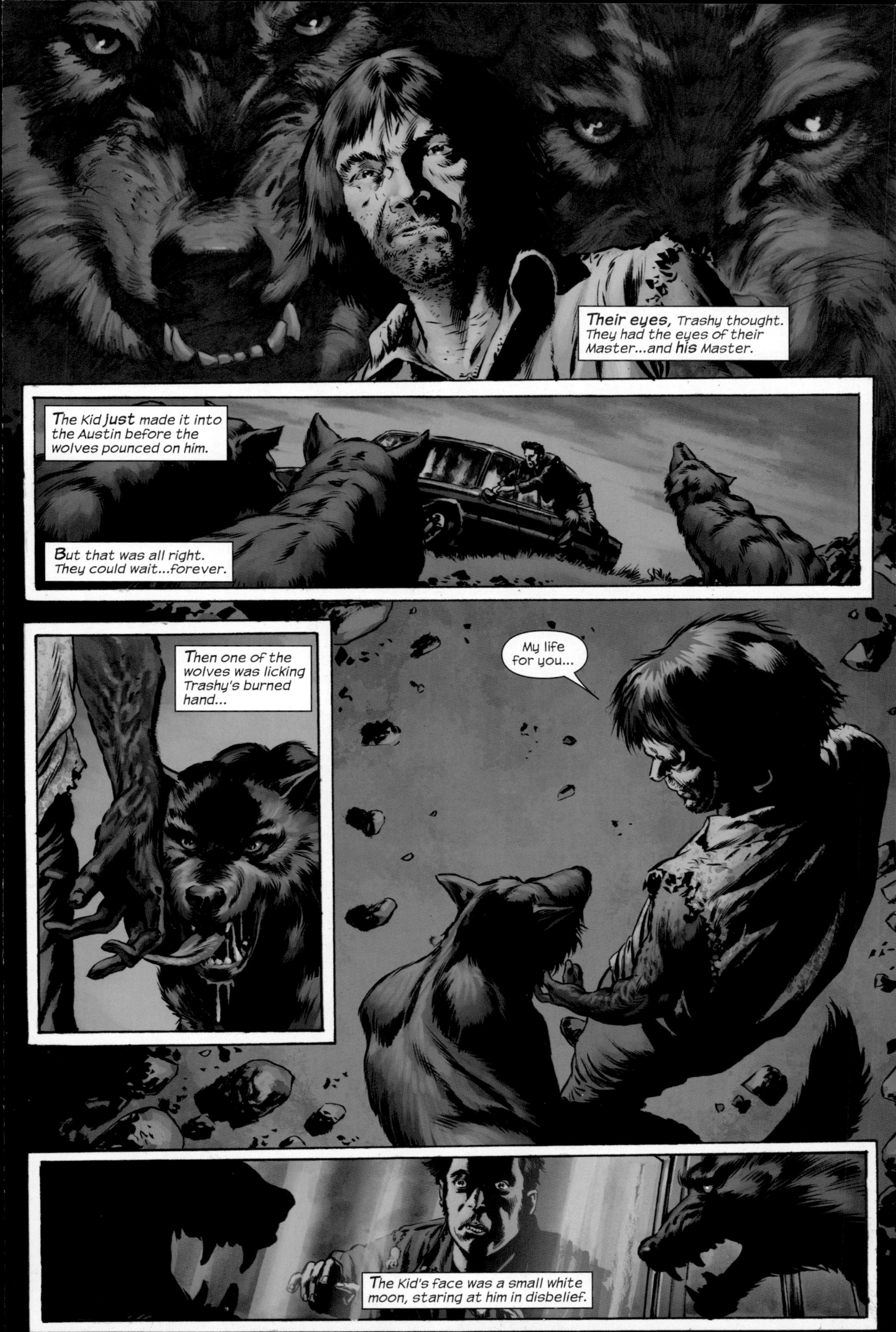
Their eyes, Trashy thought. They had the eyes of their Master...and his Master.
The Kid just made it into the Austin before the wolves pounced on him.
But that was all right. They could wait...forever.
Then one of the wolves was licking Trashy's burned hand...
My life for you...
The Kid's face was a small white moon, staring at him in disbelief.

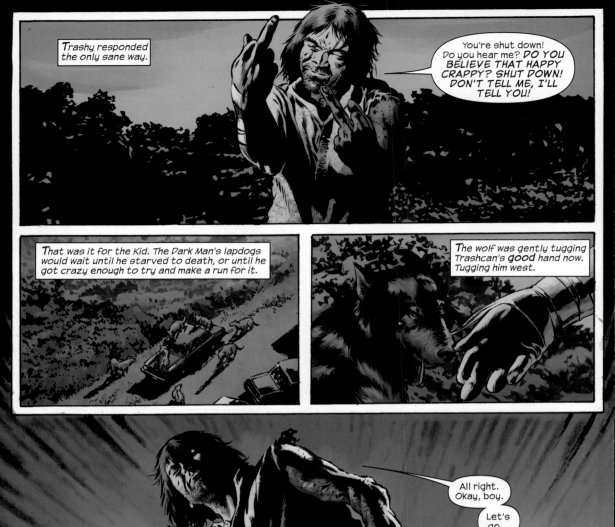

Trashy responded the only sane way.

You're shut down! Do you hear me? *DO YOU BELIEVE THAT HAPPY CRAPPY? SHUT DOWN! DON'T TELL ME, I'LL TELL YOU!*

That was it for the Kid. The Dark Man's lapdogs would wait until he starved to death, or until he got crazy enough to try and make a run for it.

The wolf was gently tugging Trashcan's *good* hand now. Tugging him west.

All right. Okay, boy.

Let's go...

By the time Trashcan Man made it through the Eisenhower Tunnel, his gray-ghostly guardians had faded away. Almost...evaporated.

But it didn't matter. He had seen the Dark Man's hand at work, had seen it plain, and he was too exalted to do anything but pray and keep moving.

The beauty of religious mania is that it has the power to explain everything.

Which is perhaps why (and how) Trashy spent twenty minutes talking to a crow on the road west of Vail, convinced it was an emissary of the Dark Man...

...or the Dark Man himself.

By late July, Trashy was speeding across western Utah on the I-15, which runs all the way to San Bernardino.

And when the front wheel of his bike parted company from the rest of the machine, and Trashy was pitched over the handlebars and split his head open, he kept walking, kept shuffling...

Cii-a-bo-la, my life for you, Ci-a-bola, bumpty, bumpty, bump...

And so it was almost dawn on the morning of August 5 when Trashcan Man, once Donald Merwin Elbert, entered Cibola, otherwise known as Vegas.

Missing a shoe he'd lost somewhere in the desert.

He saw many things, but he didn't stop until he reached the MGM Grand Hotel...

...or, more specifically, the working fountain in front of the hotel.

He could feel the pores of his body open like a million mouths and slurp the water in like a sponge.

Cibola! Cibola! My life for yours!

He dogpaddled around the fountain, and drank until he was sloshing around like a filled goatskin.

It had been worth it. It had all...been...

...Trash fell instantly asleep.

And was soon surrounded by a trio of men.

Ken DeMott:

What do we do with him?

Lloyd Henreid:

Let him sleep. Flagg wants him.

Hector Drogan:

Yeah? Where the hell *is* Flagg, anyway?

You that anxious to see him, Hec?

N-no. Hey, Lloyd, you know I didn't--

Sure, I know you didn't.

Flagg will be around soon. He's been waiting for this guy. This guy...

...he's something special.

On the grass, oblivious to all this, Trashcan Man slept on.

chapter
TWO

WARNING
BIOLOGICAL
ARD

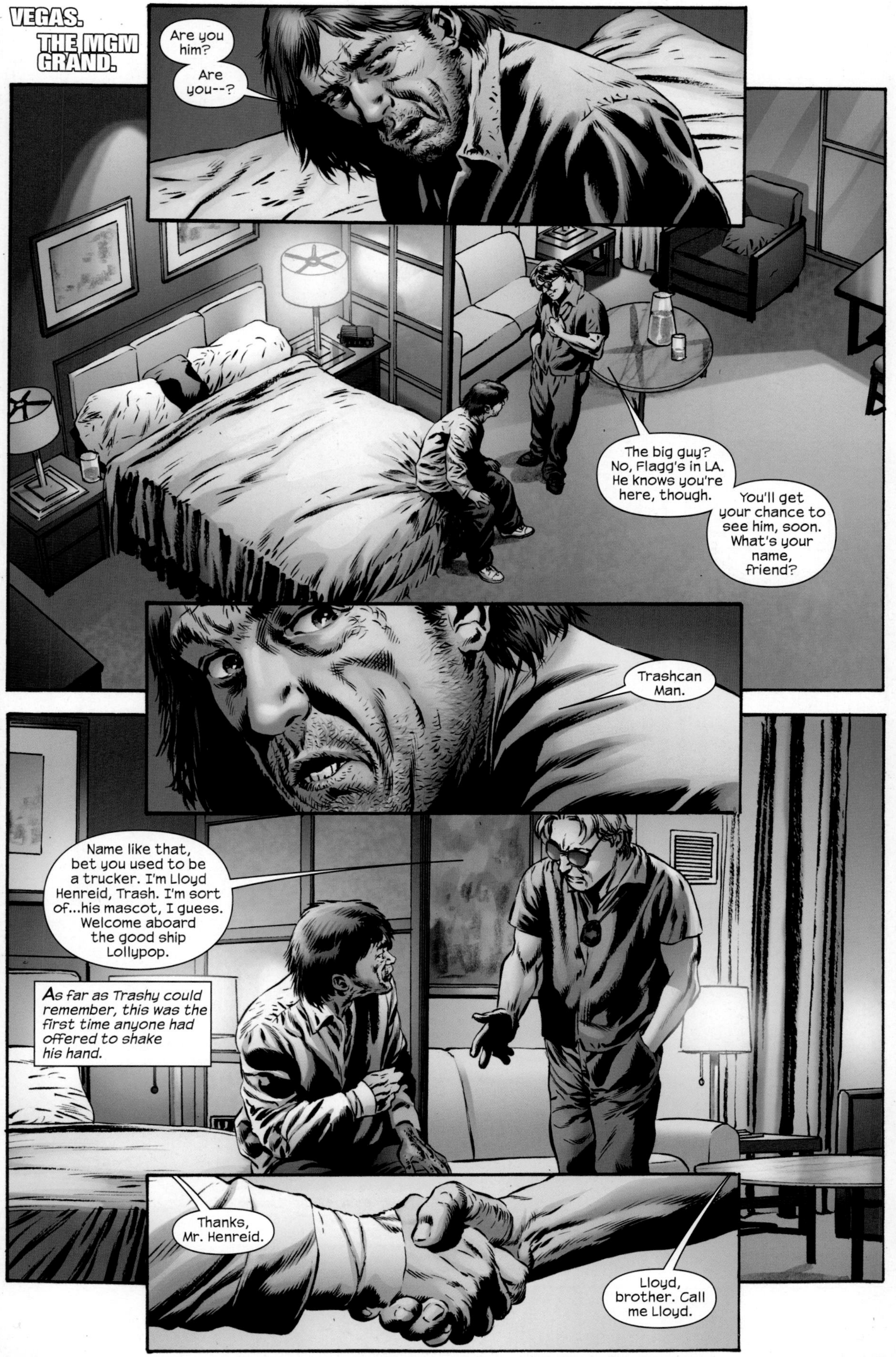
VEGAS.
THE MGM GRAND.
Are you him?
Are you--?
The big guy? No, Flagg's in LA. He knows you're here, though.
You'll get your chance to see him, soon. What's your name, friend?
Trashcan Man.
Name like that, bet you used to be a trucker. I'm Lloyd Henreid, Trash. I'm sort of...his mascot, I guess. Welcome aboard the good ship Lollypop.
As far as Trashy could remember, this was the first time anyone had offered to shake his hand.
Thanks, Mr. Henreid.
Lloyd, brother. Call me Lloyd.

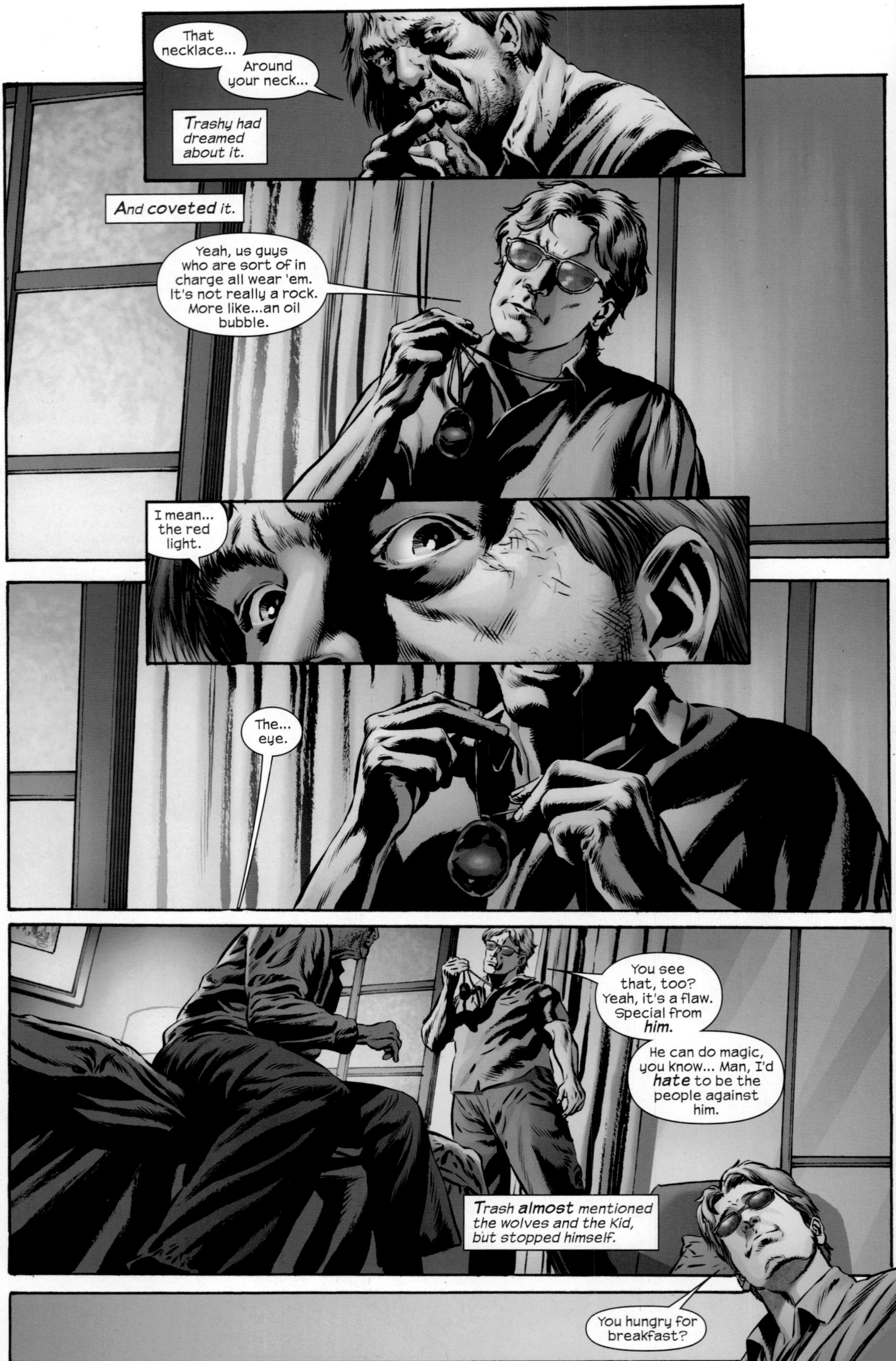
That necklace...
Around your neck...
Trashy had dreamed about it.
And coveted it.
Yeah, us guys who are sort of in charge all wear 'em. It's not really a rock. More like...an oil bubble.
I mean... the red light.
The... eye.
You see that, too? Yeah, it's a flaw. Special from him.
He can do magic, you know... Man, I'd hate to be the people against him.
Trash almost mentioned the wolves and the Kid, but stopped himself.
You hungry for breakfast?

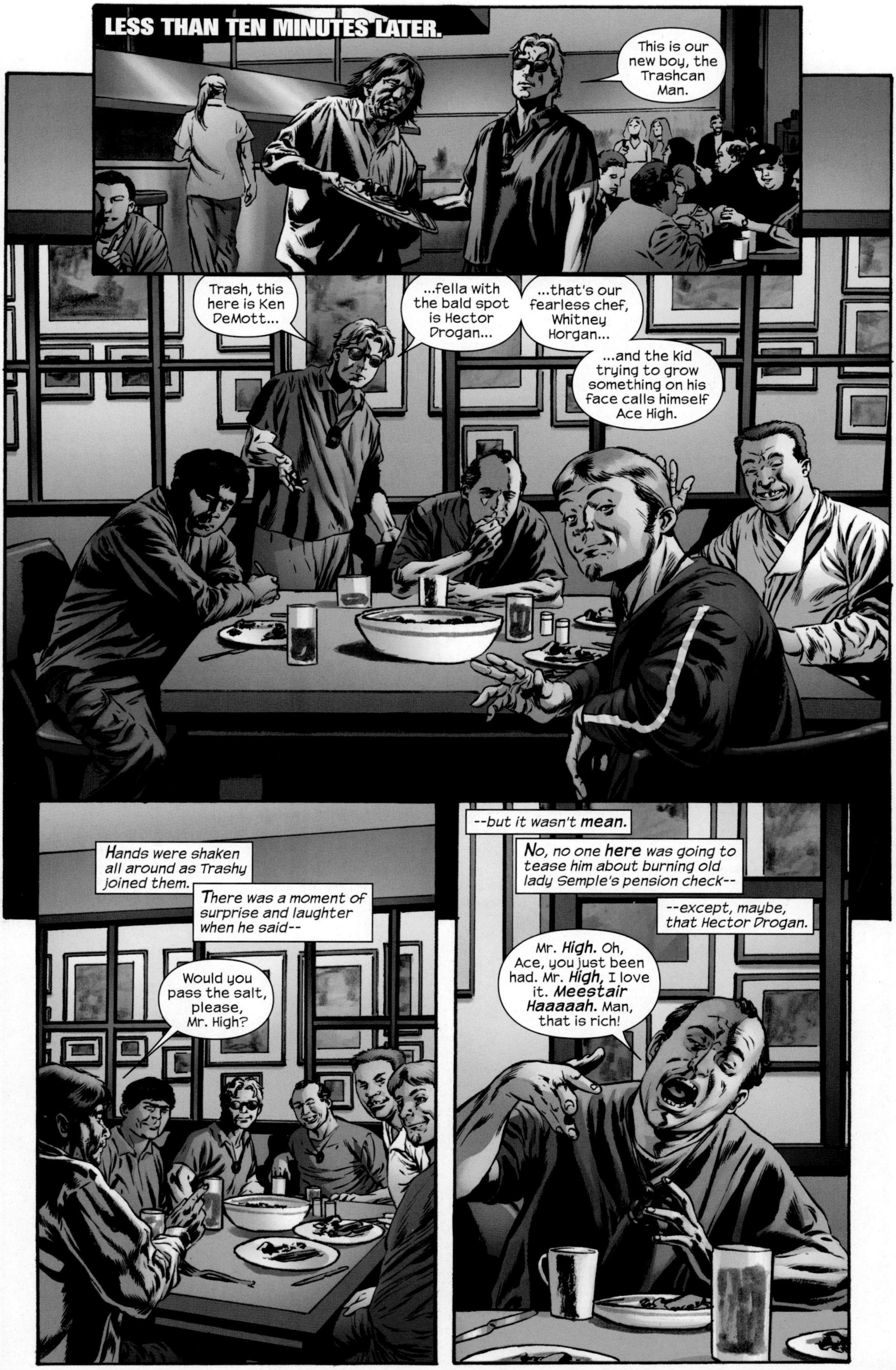
LESS THAN TEN MINUTES LATER.
This is our new boy, the Trashcan Man.
Trash, this here is Ken DeMott...
...fella with the bald spot is Hector Drogan...
...that's our fearless chef, Whitney Horgan...
...and the kid trying to grow something on his face calls himself Ace High.
Hands were shaken all around as Trashy joined them.
There was a moment of surprise and laughter when he said--
Would you pass the salt, please, Mr. High?
--but it wasn't mean.
No, no one here was going to tease him about burning old lady Semple's pension check--
--except, maybe, that Hector Drogan.
Mr. High. Oh, Ace, you just been had. Mr. High, I love it. Meestair Haaaaah. Man, that is rich!

Just Ace, my man. That'll get me every time.

Trashcan Man nodded, smiled, and dug into his eggs, feeling **warm** *and good inside.*

The warmth and goodness were so foreign to his nature, it almost felt like a disease.

Oh, Mr. *Hiiiiigh?* Ace, you **never** gonna live that down, I swear you won't.

Maybe not, Heck, but I'm sure-God gonna live it up!

But it wasn't a disease. It was, simply, happiness.

What a bunch of good people, Trash thought... *I'm home.*

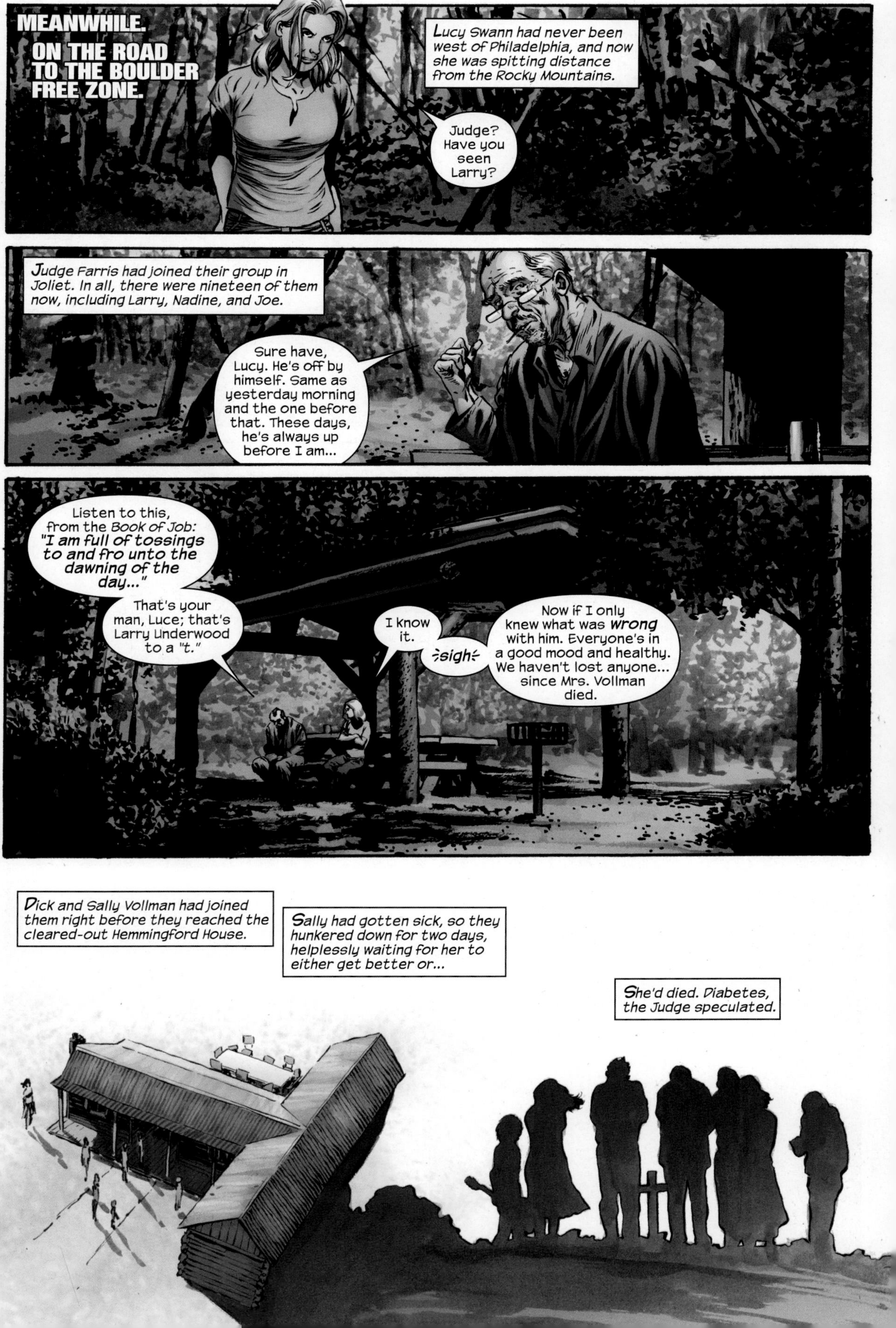
MEANWHILE.
ON THE ROAD TO THE BOULDER FREE ZONE.
Lucy Swann had never been west of Philadelphia, and now she was spitting distance from the Rocky Mountains.
Judge? Have you seen Larry?
Judge Farris had joined their group in Joliet. In all, there were nineteen of them now, including Larry, Nadine, and Joe.
Sure have, Lucy. He's off by himself. Same as yesterday morning and the one before that. These days, he's always up before I am...
Listen to this, from the Book of Job: "I am full of tossings to and fro unto the dawning of the day..."
That's your man, Luce; that's Larry Underwood to a "t."
I know it.
sigh
Now if I only knew what was wrong with him. Everyone's in a good mood and healthy. We haven't lost anyone... since Mrs. Vollman died.
Dick and Sally Vollman had joined them right before they reached the cleared-out Hemmingford House.
Sally had gotten sick, so they hunkered down for two days, helplessly waiting for her to either get better or...
She'd died. Diabetes, the Judge speculated.

Larry, it strikes me, is a man who found himself comparatively late in life.

Men like that are rarely *sure,* and when something goes wrong--say, a Mrs. Vollman dying--they blame themselves.

I think there's something more...

What was that quote? *"I am full of tossings and turnings unto the dawning of the day?"*

That's it.

Pretty good description of a man in love, isn't it?

Before the Judge could reply, Lucy was drifting away, back towards the others. She would talk to Larry later.

Women know.

Women almost *always* know...

Trashy had been bussed up to the Boulder Dam.

He spent most of the day wrapping copper wire around the spindles of burned-out motors...

...drinking in a *glorious* view of the lake from his bench.

No one supervised him, and he assumed it was because everyone *must* be as in love with what they were doing as he was, himself.

He was thinking he should get a large book and write some of his thoughts about *him*, the Dark Man, down...

...a book of psalms of praise...

...when Ken DeMott arrived:

Come on, Trashy. Work's over. We're going back to Vegas. Everyone. The buses are waiting.

Huh? Why?

I don't know, it's *his* order. Lloyd passed it along. Best not to ask questions when the hardcase is involved.

Riding a school bus back into Vegas, Trashy overheard two men talking:

It's Heck. Heck Drogan. How the hell does that spook find things out?

Shut up--

--*people* can hear you...

Trash averted his gaze and looked out the window, at the passing desert...

Once again, he was troubled in his mind.

In Vegas, everyone had gathered around the fountain. More than four hundred people, six and seven deep--

There you are, Trash. I been looking for you--

We need help and you're drafted--

What, Lloyd, what is it?

But then Trash saw Whitney Horgan and what he was guarding...

What is this? I heard something about Heck--

Go on, Whitney, radio to bring him out--

Yeah, it's Heck. He's been freebasing.

God, I *hate* these things...

You... We...nail him up?

Is *that* what this is about?

You know, I got something for you. *He* gave it to me to give to you. I can't make you take it, but...

...*do* you want it?

Take this and you take everything, Lloyd's eyes said. And what's a part of everything? Why, Heck and that crosstree and that hole in the ground, of course...

Trash thought: This is my last chance to be Donald Merwin Elbert...

He thought: I offered him my life, but this is my soul...

But, in truth, the time for choices had long since passed. Hadn't he walked halfway across the country for the Dark Man? And hadn't the Dark Man saved him from the Kid?

In for a penny, in for a pound, thought Trashcan Man.

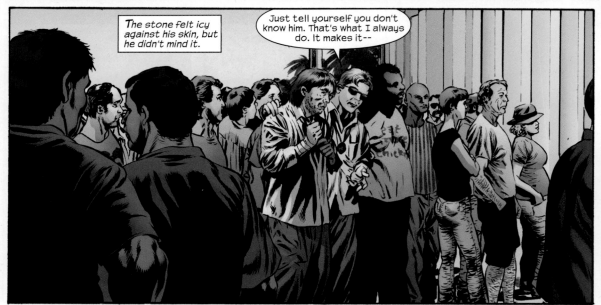

The stone felt icy against his skin, but he didn't mind it.

Just tell yourself you don't know him. That's what I always do. It makes it--

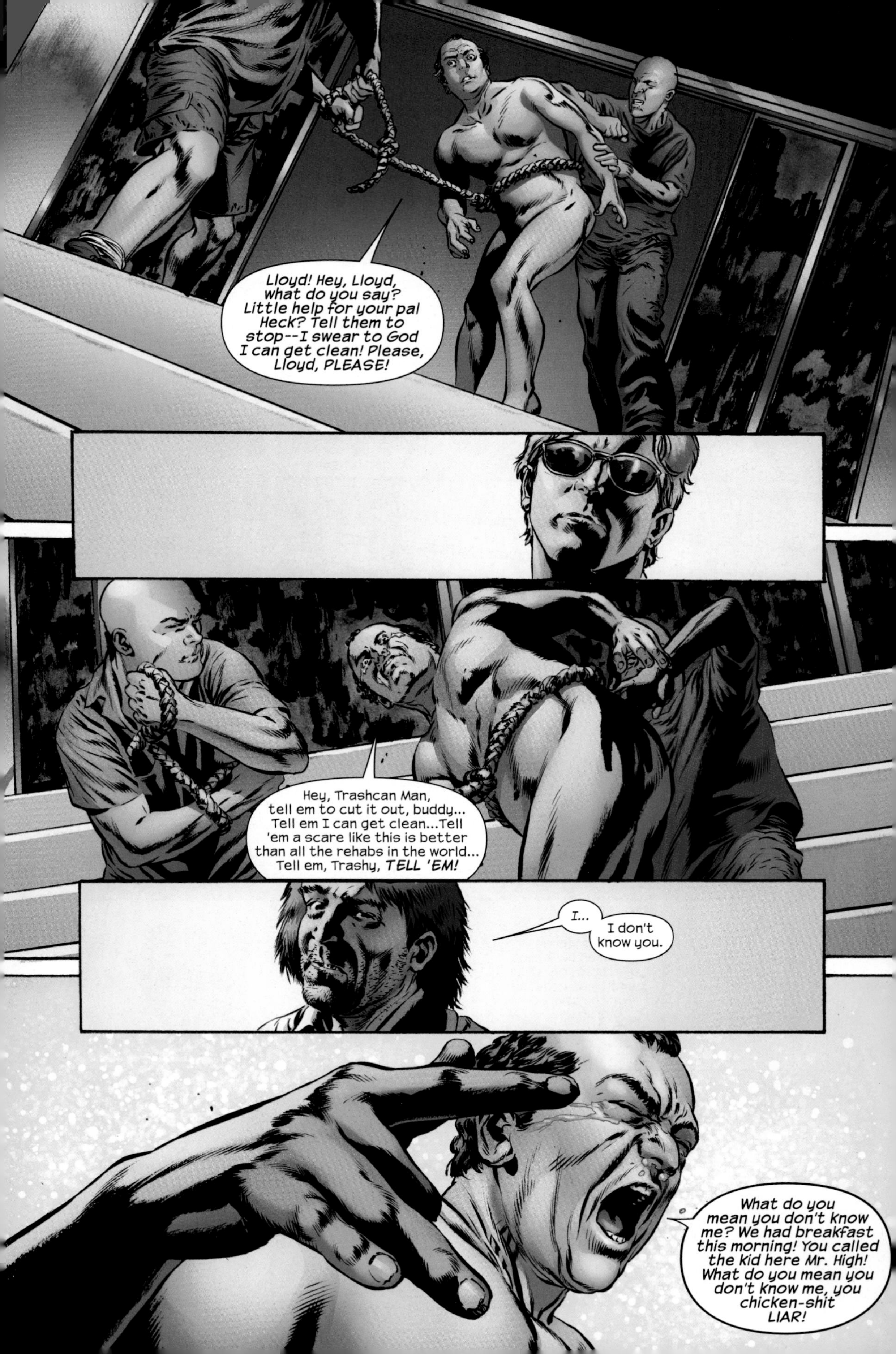
Lloyd! Hey, Lloyd, what do you say? Little help for your pal Heck? Tell them to stop--I swear to God I can get clean! Please, Lloyd, PLEASE!
Hey, Trashcan Man, tell em to cut it out, buddy... Tell em I can get clean...Tell 'em a scare like this is better than all the rehabs in the world... Tell em, Trashy, TELL 'EM!
I... I don't know you.
What do you mean you don't know me? We had breakfast this morning! You called the kid here Mr. High! What do you mean you don't know me, you chicken-shit LIAR!

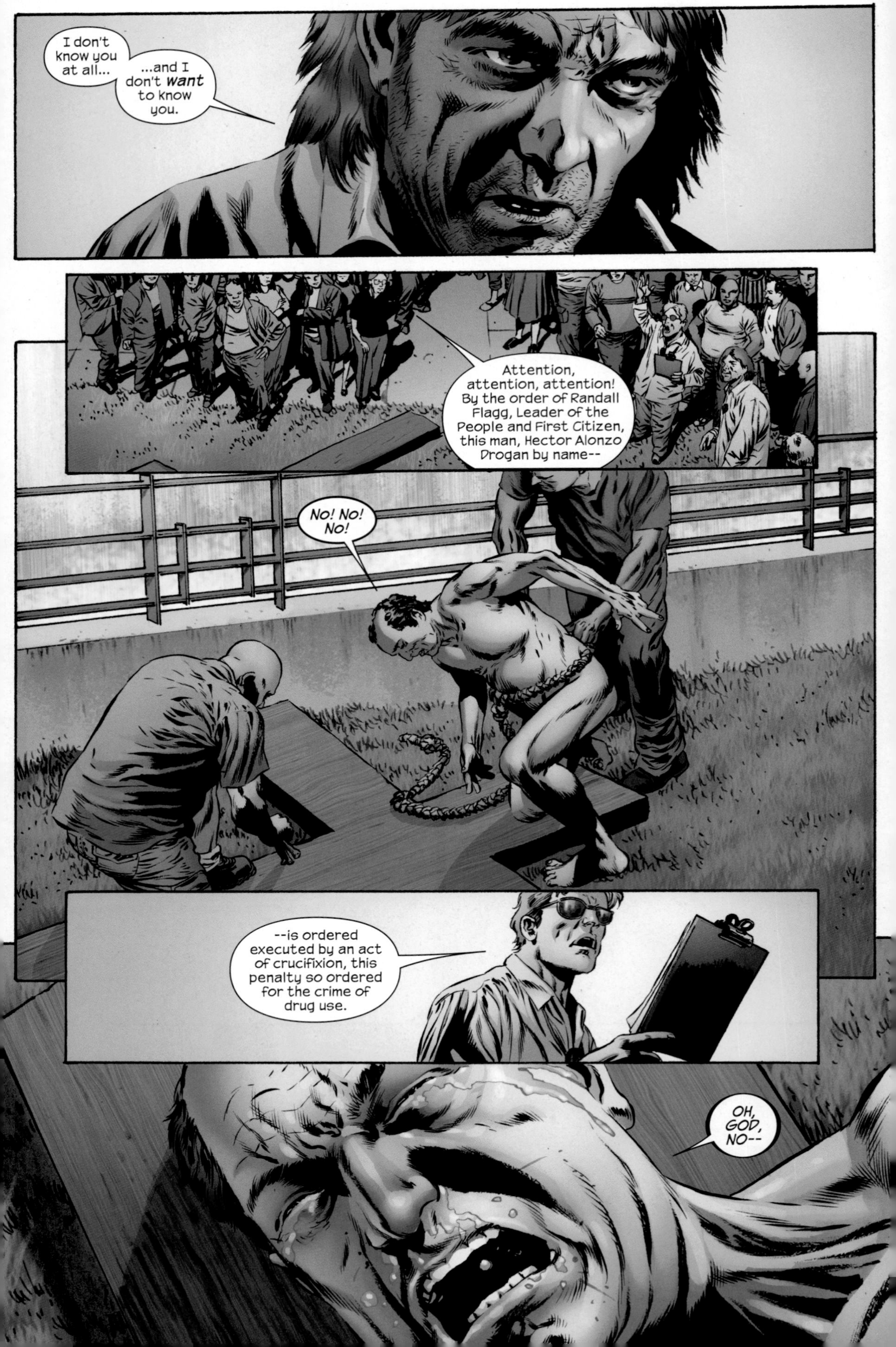
I don't know you at all...
...and I don't *want* to know you.
Attention, attention, attention! By the order of Randall Flagg, Leader of the People and First Citizen, this man, Hector Alonzo Drogan by name--
No! No! No!
--is ordered executed by an act of crucifixion, this penalty so ordered for the crime of drug use.
OH, GOD, NO--

At Lloyd's instruction, Trashy was one of the men charged with holding Hector down while Whitey Horgan nailed him to the cross...

Drug use is not allowed in this Society of the People because it impairs the user's ability to contribute fully to the Society of the People. Specifically in this case, the accused Hector Drogan was found with a supply of cocaine.

Oh, my God, it hurts! Oh my God, my God, oh God, God, God--

The cool stone against Trashy's skin reassured him...

...please...

...oh, God...

...please, *please*...

This communication ends with a solemn warning to the people of Las Vegas. Let this bill of true facts be nailed above the miscreant's head, marked with the seal of the First Citizen, Randall Flagg by name.

The crowd remained assembled for almost an hour, each person afraid to be the first to leave.

*Trashcan Man wasn't frightened, though. Why **should** he have been? He hadn't known the dead man.*

He hadn't known him at all.

THAT NIGHT.
ACROSS THE
COLORADO BORDER.

Larry? Room for me?

.... Sure.

By Lucy's estimation, they would reach Boulder tomorrow.

If they got an early enough start, they might even make it to the Boulder Free Zone (which is what the man on the radio called it) in time for lunch.

The idea to find and use a CB radio to get in touch with other survivors had been Nadine's, and it was a good one...

This is Ralph Brentner, Boulder Free Zone. If you hear me, reply on Channel Fourteen. Repeat, Channel Fourteen--

Penny for your thoughts?

They...they're mostly about Nadine.

She's acting like she's coming unraveled, Larry, do you know what I mean?

Larry stiffened. He *did* know.

By the time they'd reached Hemmingford House, there were brown circles under Nadine's eyes from not sleeping. Her magnificent hair was noticeably whiter. And if anyone touched her, she jumped. *Flinched.*

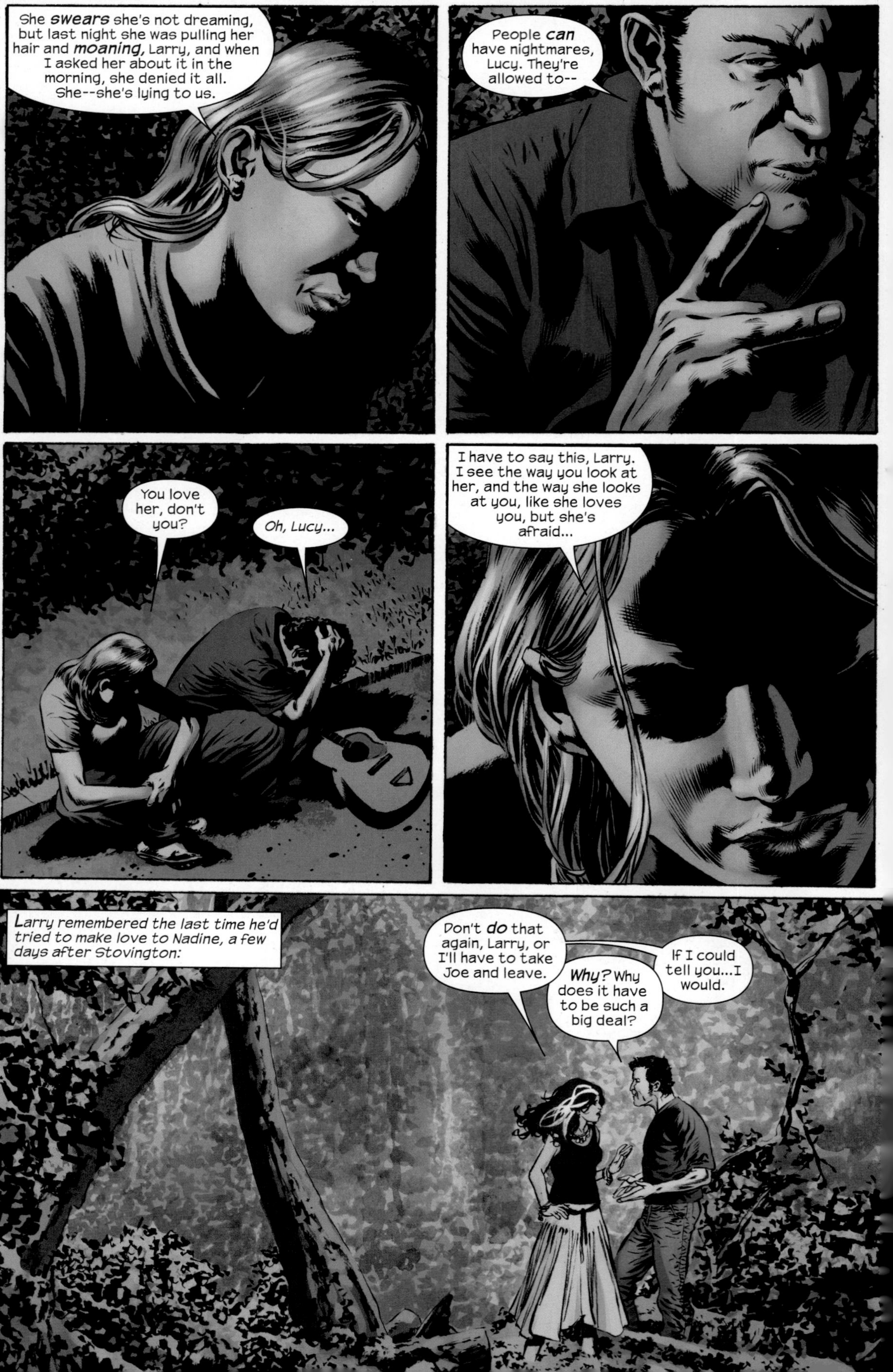
She **swears** she's not dreaming, but last night she was pulling her hair and **moaning,** Larry, and when I asked her about it in the morning, she denied it all. She--she's lying to us.
People **can** have nightmares, Lucy. They're allowed to--
You love her, don't you?
Oh, Lucy...
I have to say this, Larry. I see the way you look at her, and the way she looks at you, like she loves you, but she's afraid...
Larry remembered the last time he'd tried to make love to Nadine, a few days after Stovington:
Don't **do** that again, Larry, or I'll have to take Joe and leave.
Why? Why does it have to be such a big deal?
If I could tell you...I would.

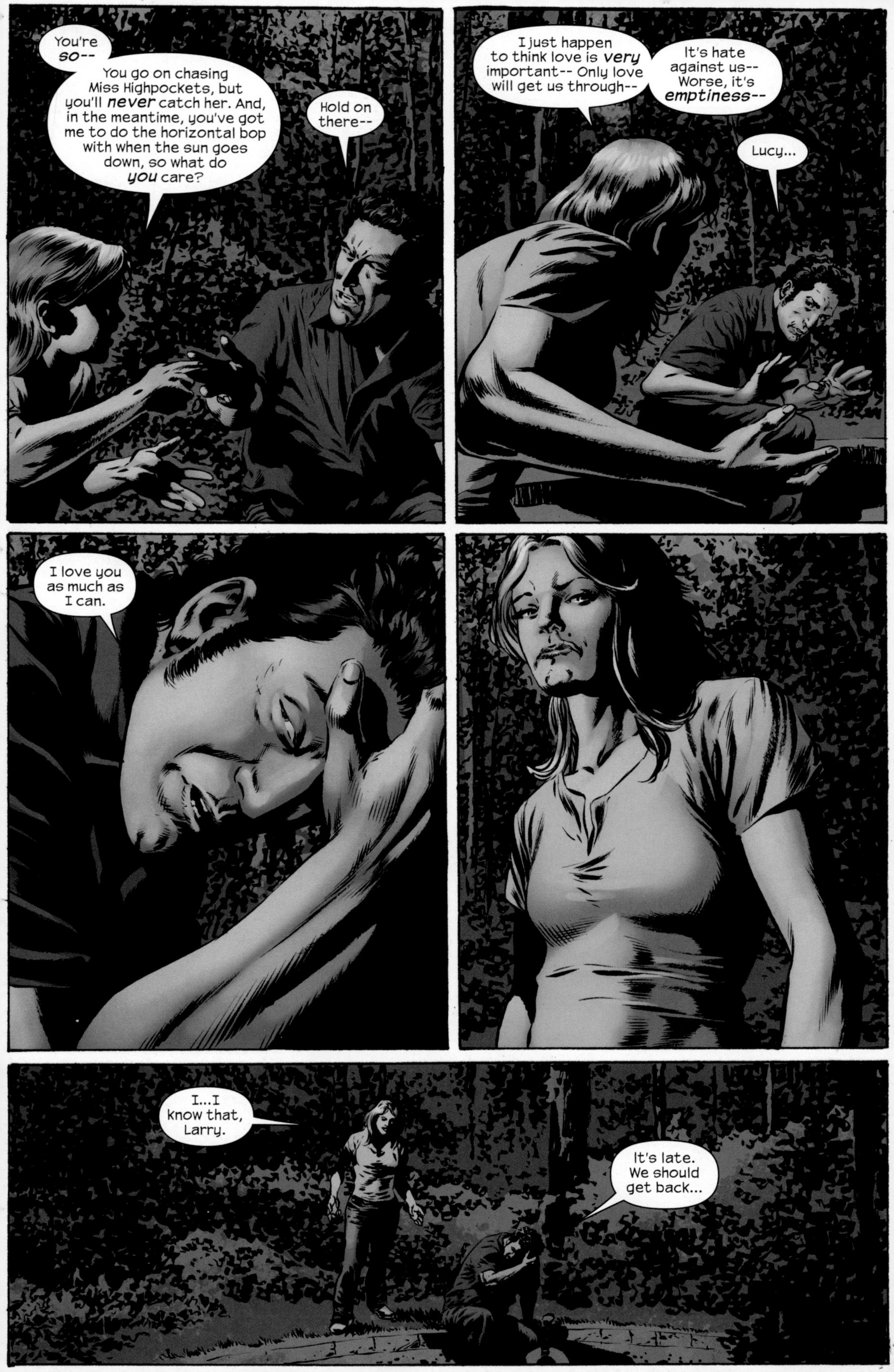
You're so--
You go on chasing Miss Highpockets, but you'll never catch her. And, in the meantime, you've got me to do the horizontal bop with when the sun goes down, so what do you care?
Hold on there--
I just happen to think love is very important-- Only love will get us through--
It's hate against us-- Worse, it's emptiness--
Lucy...
I love you as much as I can.
I...I know that, Larry.
It's late. We should get back...

THAT NIGHT, AT CAMP.

Nadine came awake like a cat twenty minutes after Larry and Lucy finished their act of half-hearted love and fell asleep.

Someone wants me...

There's that. Someone wants me, it's true.

But...it's so cold.

Nadine's parents and brother had been killed when she was six. They'd gone on a family trip, and she'd stayed behind.

It was all right. She'd been adopted, and never felt like she belonged to anyone but herself. She was the earth's child.

She went to live with an aunt and uncle in the White Mountains of New Hampshire.

The night she turned sixteen was a lovenight. And as a boy chased her under the moon, across the dewy grass, she thought if he caught her, she would give him whatever prize he wanted...

*...but he **hadn't** caught her.*

That was the night she realized that she had to wait for her intended. Her...dark bridegroom.

That was the night, she believed, that her hair started to whiten.

Where had he been when she was sixteen? On what streets, what back roads? What cold winds were his?

She was only sure that he was an orphan like her, that he was an American man with a taste for apple pie, and that his ways were the secret ways.

After college, she rented a cottage with two other girls and buried herself in her work.

She supposed they called her a spinster-in-waiting, perhaps even speculated she was a lesbian, but she wasn't. She was simply...unbroken. Waiting.

Every so often, she would *feel* it... She'd be picking up toys in an empty classroom, and it would occur to her:

A change is coming... A great wind is going to blow...

And the change *had* come. And in her dreams, she had begun to *know* her bridegroom, to understand him...

He was the one she had been waiting for. And she *wanted* to go to him, but...

...he *terrified* her.

She felt like the prize ring in a tug-of-war rope.

She knew her purity was important to the Dark Man, But she *was* also attracted to Larry.

Larry, who was like an optical illusion, where the water looks an inch or two deep, but when you put your hand in, you're suddenly wet to the shoulder...

As they moved west, picking up survivors, her hope that it would end for her without confrontation had gradually died.

The others had been having opposing dreams: The old woman and the Dark Man.

Nadine had never dreamed of **her**. And as the others stopped dreaming of the Dark Man, **hers** only intensified, and she started to **know** things about him.

His name was Randall Flagg, for instance, and those who opposed him were either crucified or banished into the boiling sink of Death Valley...

Boulder was her last hope. Boulder and the old woman and her people. They were the good guys.

Playing over and over in her, like a dominant chord, was the belief that murder in this decimated world was the **gravest** sin...and the awful certainty that **death** was Randall Flagg's business.

But oh, how she wanted his cold kiss...

A shooting star scratched its fire across the sky, and like a child, Nadine wished on it...

You're dressed, good. It's time, Trashy. He wants to see you, now.

Goosebumps rashed out on Trashy's sunburned arms.

Where is he?

My life for him, oh, yes--

Top floor.

He got in after we finished burning Drogan's body.

Four minutes later, they were in the elevator, riding up.

No one ever sees him come or go, Trash, but they always know when he's taken off. And when he's come back.

On the top floor, Trash stepped off; Lloyd did not.

Aren't you--?

No, he wants to see you alone. Good luck, Trash.

Trashy found himself in a dark, sumptuous hallway, and at the end of it...

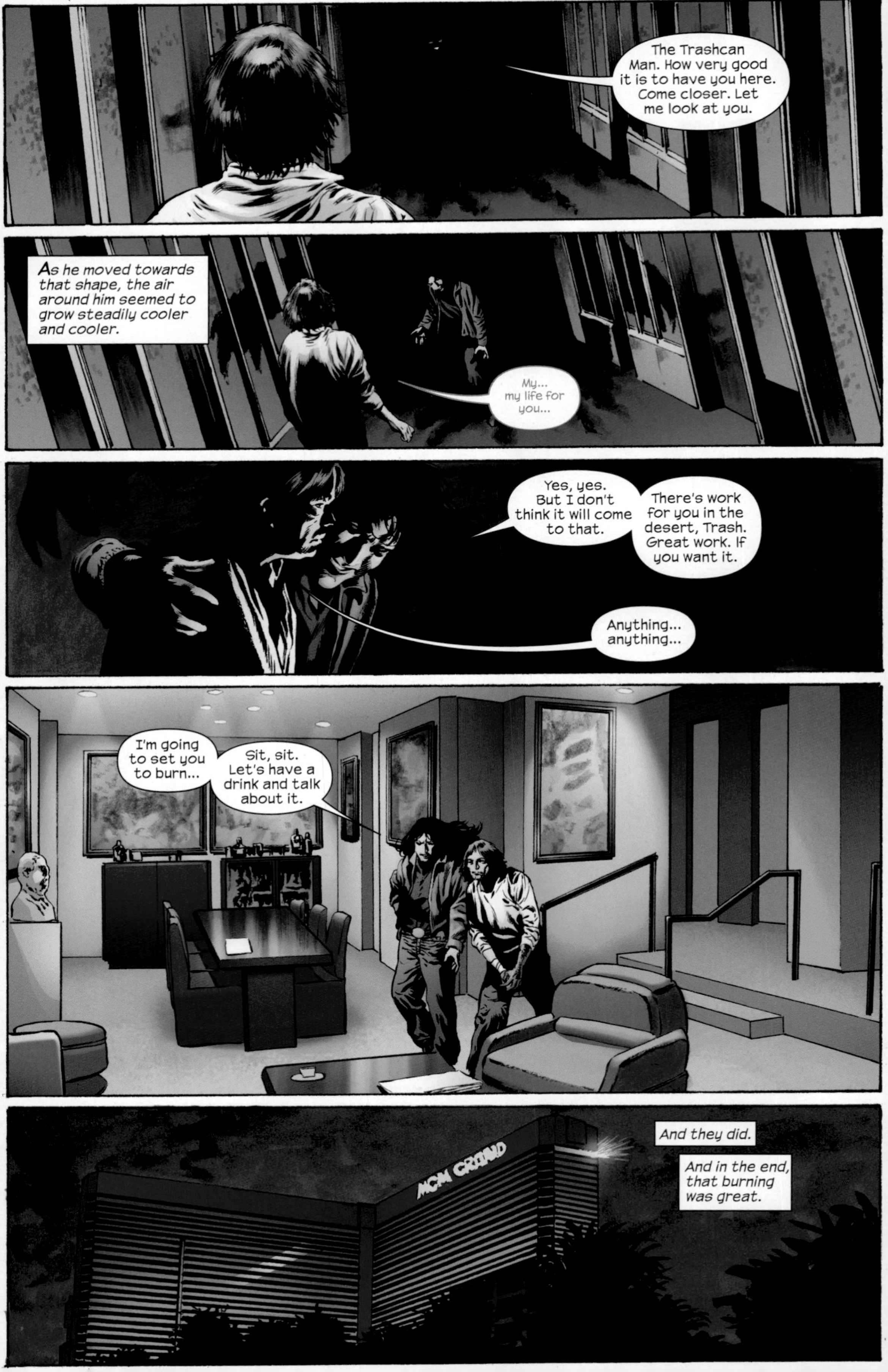
The Trashcan Man. How very good it is to have you here. Come closer. Let me look at you.
As he moved towards that shape, the air around him seemed to grow steadily cooler and cooler.
My... my life for you...
Yes, yes. But I don't think it will come to that.
There's work for you in the desert, Trash. Great work. If you want it.
Anything... anything...
I'm going to set you to burn...
Sit, sit. Let's have a drink and talk about it.
MGM GRAND
And they did.
And in the end, that burning was great.

chapter
THREE

WARNING

BIOLOGICAL
RD

DAWN.
OVER THE BOULDER FREE ZONE.

"I am going to have a *hell* of a headache this afternoon, Stu. I don't believe I've stayed up drinking all night since I was an undergrad."

"This sunrise is worth it, Glen."

"Beautiful...You ever been in the Rockies before?"

"Nope. But I'm glad I came...What's going to happen now?"

"Happen?"

"That's why I got you up here. I told Frannie, 'I'm gonna get Glen good and drunk and then pick his brains about what happens next.'"

Society. Society happens next...People are coming in dribs and drabs right now, but there may be as many as eight thousand by the first snow in November.

Write that down as prediction number one.

We suspect there's an Adversary, the Dark Man that we dream about, west of us somewhere, on the other side of the Rockies...

I think he's going to get most of the techies coming to him...

We may end up with more people--I like to believe most people are inherently good and, therefore, *drawn* to good-- but he'll end up with the folks who like their trains to run on time...

I tell you, Stu. At night, when the sun goes down, I think of the Adversary and his team, busy as bees, getting the power back up, dusting the missile silos and tanks and helicopters off...

...and I get scared.

Me, too. We've *got* to start getting *our* shit together, Glen.

Or we'll wake up some morning to find that hardcase *waltzing* into Boulder at the head of an armored column, complete with air support.

Not tomorrow, but maybe by May.

So let's start getting it together...

You talk, I'll write.

We re-create America, by means fair and foul. Government comes first.

We call a town hall meeting for everyone to attend.

Before that, we form an ad hoc Organization Committee of...seven, let's say. You, me, Andros, Fran, Harold maybe, a couple more. We set the agenda for the meeting.

Like?

First, reading and ratification of the *Declaration of Independence*, the *Constitution*, and the *Bill of Rights*.

It's very important that we ratify the *spirit* of the old society ASAP...

Go on.

The next item would be that we run the government like a New England township, a perfect democracy, with seven...call 'em Free Zone Representatives.

And we'll see to it that those seven are the same as on the ad hoc committee.

Uh-*huh*.

What then?

We vote that Mother Abagail is to be given absolute veto power over the Board. Whether or not she agrees, or will ever use that power, we can't expect to have a workable government here unless *she's* its titular head...

"She's the thing we all have in common... The people coming here dreamed of her; she's what makes us feel safe and secure..."

Mother Abagail was thinking about electricity.

And about how Hemmingford Home, with its pump and all, was better equipped to handle the end of the world than this fancy house in the Mapleton Hill section of Boulder...

They would get the power back on, of course. It was one of the things God had shown her in her dreams.

She knew a goodish number of things that were coming; some from the dreams, some from her common sense.

Soon, all the people would stop running around like headless chickens and start pulling together.

She wasn't a sociologist like Glen Bateman, but she knew people always did pull together after awhile.

The curse and the blessing of the human race was its chumminess...

They'll want to form some kind of government, she thought. Probably, they'll want to run it around me...

She couldn't allow *that*, of course, much as she would like to; *that* would not be God's will.

She would insist Nick have a part in the running of things, and Ralph, and *maybe* that Texan Stuart Redman.

They might also want that fat boy she didn't like: Harold.

(The way he was always **grinning**, she thought he must be keeping some kind of secret. Some nasty, **stinking** thing in his heart...)

If that was the case, she wouldn't **say** anything. Her place in their councils and deliberations had only to do with the Dark Man.

He had no name, although it pleased him to call himself Flagg for the time being; she knew that.

Also, that on the far side of the mountains his work was already well begun.

She didn't know his specific plans-- they were as veiled as whatever secrets lay in that fat boy's heart-- but she was certain of his goal:

To destroy all of them.

The black man who, unlike God and man, was only able to **break** and unshape...

Anti-Christ? Call him *anti-creation*...

He would have his followers, of course. He was a liar; his father was the Father of Lies; and he would be like a big neon sign to the cowardly and the wicked...

Would they win? Would *he*?

God was a gamesman; it was not for her to know.

Thy will be done.

Mother? There's some folks that just got here and would like to say howdy, if you ain't too tired. A pretty good crew, I'd say. Fella in charge is named Underwood.

Ralph Brentner, who was part of Nick's team.

Bring 'em up, Ralph, that's fine.

Good enough, Mother; will do.

Before you go, Ralph, where's Nick? Haven't seen him today nor yesterday neither. He getting too good for homefolks?

He's been out at the reservoir. Him and that electrician, Brad Kichner, have been looking at the power plant. I was out there earlier.

Figured all those chiefs orta have at least one Indian to boss around...

That made Mother Abagail cackle; she did like Ralph, didn't she?

Anyway, that fella Redman came by while we were workin'. To talk to Nick about being on some committee.

Nick wrote a couple of pages, but what it came down to was...fine by me, if it's fine by Mother Abagail. We'll do whatever she wants.

What I *want* is to go on livin' free like I always have, like an *American*. I just want my say when it's time for me to have it. Like an *American*.

Well, you'll have all of that.

Nick and Stu asked me to print up seven hundred flyers for this meeting they're planning. I told 'em I'd find the biggest hand-crank mimeograph I could.

That's fine. Time everyone got done *lollygaggin'* around--

Speaking of which, people out by the gate, getting heatstroke, while you and me chin like there's no tomorrow...

I'll bring them in.

And Ralph?

Print a thousand.

The new arrivals filed in, a group of nineteen, and Mother Abagail felt her sin, the **mother** of sin.

Pride.

The female side of Satan in the human race, the quiet egg of all sin...Pride, which had kept Moses out of Canaan...

She had always been a proud woman. Proud of the floor she washed on her hands and knees, proud her children had turned out all right, proud of her life. But...

...she had not **made** her life. And the **mothers** of children were the **daughters** of God, don't forget.

And on this fine morning, as the pilgrims filed through her gate, she thought, proudly, It's me they've come to see.

I am Abagail Freemantle, but most folks round here call me Mother Abagail.

You're really real.

I'm...We're glad to be here. My name's Larry Underwood. I... I dreamed of you.

She thought this man seemed a bit green and apt to bend, but...she liked him.

I'm Lucy Swann, Mother Abagail, pleased to make your acquaintance.

I dreamed of you, too, and would you mind if I asked, well...

A hundred and eight at last count, though it feels like two hundred and sixteen some days. Glad you could come by, Lucy.

Then it was a boy and a woman with dark eyes.

The boy was all right, but the woman...

He's here, she thought. *He's come in the shape of this woman...*

For behold he comes in more forms than his own...the wolf...the crow...the snake...

For Nadine Cross, the moment was one of confusion.

An almost swooning sense of revulsion and terror came over her because the old woman could...*what?*

Could see:

He's in her--
the Devil's Imp.

Nadine thought:

All of their power
is right here...She's
all they've got,
although they may
think differently.

Hello.
I'm Nadine
Cross.

I know
who you
are.

This is Joe.
Do you know
him, as well?

I don't think
Joe's his name any
more than mine's
Cassandra...and I
don't think you're
his mom.

What's
your name,
chap?

He won't...
or *can't*...
tell you.

I don't
think he
remembers--

*Leo
Rockway,*
that's me!

I'm Leo!

Come away, Joe. She's old. You'll hurt her. She's very old and...*not very strong.*

That's not my name. *Leo! That's* my name!

I know who you are...

Yes. And I know you...

All right, Leo, or whatever you like. Just come away before you tire her more than she already is.

As they moved away from her, Mother Abagail's sense of revelation began to grow fuzzy...

She became unsure of what she just felt...

Why were you like that? Nadine?

I can't think... He comes in many shapes...

What happened...? I was sitting here, waiting to be kowtowed to--no use denying that--but there was something about that woman...

...wasn't there?

Hey, Mother Abagail. The name's Mark Zellman. From Lowville, New York.

I dreamed about you.

Then the thread was gone, and she was bantering again:

I had me a great-nephew lived in upstate New York. Town named...Rouse's Point, on Lake Champlain.

After Zellman, others came to make their manners.

Including an old man named Richard Farris, nicknamed the judge, who **almost** made her feel uncomfortable again.

She spoke to them all, nodded, smiled, but the pleasure was gone...

...replaced by the feeling, fading, that she had **missed** something of great significance and might later be sorry.

BASELINE DRIVE.
NICK AND RALPH'S HOUSE.

Nick thought better when he wrote, so he jotted down everything that might be of importance...

For instance, the fact that Boulder wasn't like other towns.

Oh, there were corpses here, and something would have to be done about them, but it wasn't like the other towns that stank of...of charnel houses.

It was as if, somehow, Mother Abagail had led them to the one city in the United States that was more or less clear of plague victims...

Not that it would matter much if they didn't get the power running by the time the first cold snap arrived.

If they didn't, Nick was afraid that the gathering flock would begin to slip away, and all the meetings, representatives, and ratifications wouldn't stop them.

An unpleasant feeling seemed to be running through the people gathered in Boulder. They were like a bunch of scared kids knocking around in the local haunted house after dark...

Luckily, according to Ralph, there wasn't much wrong at the power plant; possibly, they could have the lights on again by Labor Day...

Earlier today, before Ralph went upstairs to sleep, he'd given Nick a copy of the flyer...

MASS MEETING
REPRESENTATIVE BOARD
TO BE NOMINATED
AND ELECTED!

AD HOC COMMITTEE:
NICK ANDROS
STUART REDMAN
RALPH BRENTNER
GLEN BATEMAN
SUSAN STERN
FRAN GOLDSMITH
...

Ralph had tried to take his name off the flyer and put this fellow Larry Underwood on the committee, but Nick wasn't convinced. He'd have to **meet** Underwood first.

What was holding, so far, was Nick's decision to unilaterally **strike** Harold Lauder's name from the list of ad hoc committee members.

THERE'S HUNDREDS OF PEOPLE HERE NOW AND THOUSANDS MORE ON THEIR WAY IF BATEMAN'S RIGHT. BUT WHEN RALPH AND I AND MOTHER AND TOM CULLEN AND THE REST OF OUR PARTY GOT HERE, THE ONLY LIVING THINGS IN BOULDER WERE THE CATS AND THE DEER

Nick finished his journaling for the day with three words:

AUTHORITY.
ORGANIZATION.
POLITICS.

Nick wasn't knocking Lauder out of the picture because he felt Stu Redman and Glen Bateman and their team were trying to **hog** what was really **his** football...

(Though hadn't, in a way, **he** and Tom and Mother and Ralph **founded** the Boulder Free Zone?)

Alright, it wasn't **just** that; it was also...

On more than one occasion, Nick wondered if Harold Lauder might not be crazy.

It's that **grin**, he thought. I don't want to share secrets with anyone who smiles like that and looks like he isn't sleeping well at night.

Nick's body broke out in gooseflesh.

He suddenly felt that he was a part of some bizarre sewing circle of the human race. He and Redman and Bateman and Mother Abagail and Ralph and the others...

And they each had a needle and perhaps they were working together to make a warm blanket to keep off the winter chill...

...or perhaps they had only, after a brief pause, begun to make a large **shroud** for the human race, beginning at the toes and working their way up...

After making love, Stu went to sleep and Frannie sat on their porch, thinking: I'm starting to show. Not a lot yet, but enough, apparently, to warrant conversation.

Earlier, Stu told her about a chat he'd had with Glen, who advanced the idea, cautiously, that the superflu might still be around and that Fran's baby might, possibly, die upon birth.

Count on Glen Bateman for an Unsettling Thought or Two.

What would that **mean**, though?

Well, for one, that all the people left were just an epilogue to the human race, a coda, and Frannie couldn't--

Your name wouldn't happen to be Fran Goldsmith, would it?

Holy God--

Who--?

Larry Underwood, looking for Harold Lauder, bearing gifts.

The best vintage Bordeaux in this century, as my friend Rudy used to say, God rest his soul.

Also--

Paydays! Harold's favorite! But how did you know?

That's a story...

He told her about leaving New York and heading north to Maine with Rita, then...without. He told her about following Harold's signs and a trail of Payday wrappers.

Over the miles, I started to get a *sense* of Harold.

From the candy wrappers and then the carving on the beam in that barn in Ogunquit--

What carving?

Just his initials. H.L.

Larry explained how his group continued to grow, as they moved across the country, and how he became their de facto leader.

He didn't like the responsibility, he said, and the only way he managed it--whenever he doubted himself--was to ask:

What would Harold do?

He was in my head, Frannie. And his voice made me think clearly and saved our bacon *more* than a few times.

And now I'm here and I brought this wine and candy bars.

He'll... he'll be pleased.

You know, I kind of thought he might be your man...

No, he--

No, not Harold.

I should go in now...It's been nice to meet you, Larry.

What is it, Fran? Do I have it wrong about Harold?

No, just...

You make me feel as if I've treated Harold very shabbily and...and...

Can I be *blamed* for not loving him the way I do Stu?

Of course not.

Listen, I'm sorry, I surprised you, I'll go--

He's *changed!* I don't know why or how, and sometimes I think it *might* be for the better, but I don't really know... And sometimes... I'm afraid.

Of Harold?

Frannie didn't answer that one; she thought she had already said too much.

Instead, she gave Larry directions to where Harold was living, and the two parted, uneasily...

LATER THAT NIGHT.

In bed next to Stu, thinking about Harold, thinking sleep might not come tonight, Fran sat up--

Something had *moved* inside her.

Oh, glory...

She would've woken Stu if the baby were his and not Jess's; she would've shared the moment with him.

(The next baby, she thought, If there is a next baby...)

Larry Underwood and Harold Lauder were forgotten. One thought crowded all the others from Frannie's mind:

Her baby was alive...

EBEN G. FINE PARK.
HAROLD'S HOUSE.

There were more than a *thousand* stars above Harold Lauder, but they weren't lovers' stars, they were *haters'* stars, stabs from God's icepick in a sky of black velvet.

Wish-I-may-wish-I-might-have-the-wish-I-wish-tonight:

Drop dead, folks...

Looking better than ever (fitter, his skin cleared up), Harold sat with a book in his lap, a tall volume with marbled blue binding and imitation leather covers.

The journal he started to keep after reading Frannie's diary.

He'd already filled the first 60 pages, margin-to-margin, no paragraphs, a solid outpouring of hatred like pus from a skin abscess, begging the question:

Why did Harold Lauder hate so much?

Interestingly, there was a time, for an hour or a moment, when he contemplated *jettisoning* the hatred. Considered turning himself into a *new* Harold Lauder, shaped by the sharp knife of the superflu.

He had sensed, more clearly than any of the others, that people in the Free Zone were not the same as they had been before.

In the end, though, Harold knew that to seize the new opportunity for change would have been tantamount to *murdering* himself... The ghost of every humiliation he had ever suffered cried out *against* that choice....

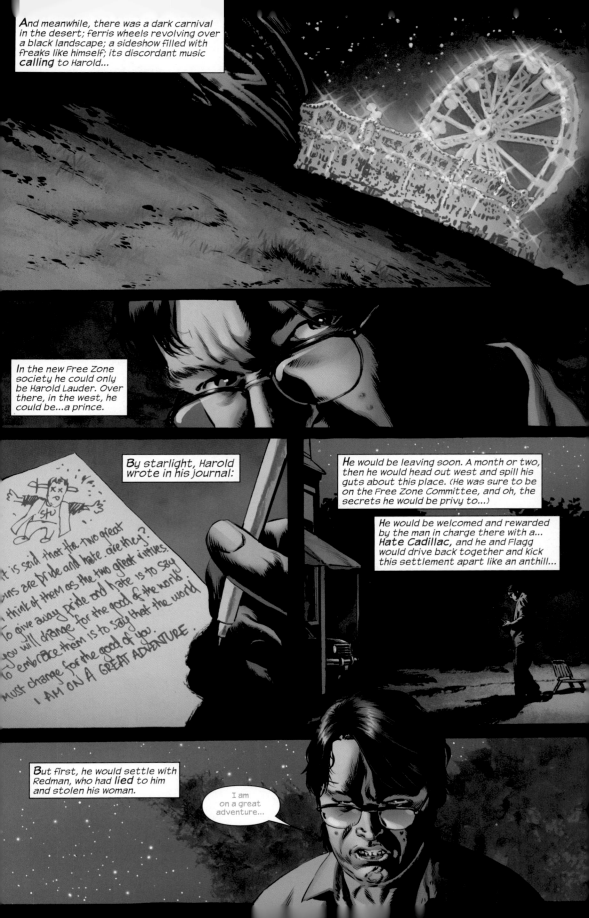

And meanwhile, there was a dark carnival in the desert; ferris wheels revolving over a black landscape; a sideshow filled with freaks like himself; its discordant music *calling* to Harold...

In the new *Free Zone* society he could only be Harold Lauder. Over there, in the west, he could be...a prince.

By starlight, Harold wrote in his journal:

It is said that the two great sins are pride and hate. Are they? I think of them as the two great virtues. To give away pride and hate is to say you will change for the good of the world. To embrace them is to say that the world must change for the good of you. I AM ON A GREAT ADVENTURE.

He would be leaving soon. A month or two, then he would head out west and spill his guts about this place. (He was sure to be on the Free Zone Committee, and oh, the secrets he would be privy to...)

He would be welcomed and rewarded by the man in charge there with a... *Hate Cadillac*, and he and Flagg would drive back together and kick this settlement apart like an anthill...

But first, he would settle with Redman, who had *lied* to him and stolen his woman.

I am on a great adventure...

chapter FOUR

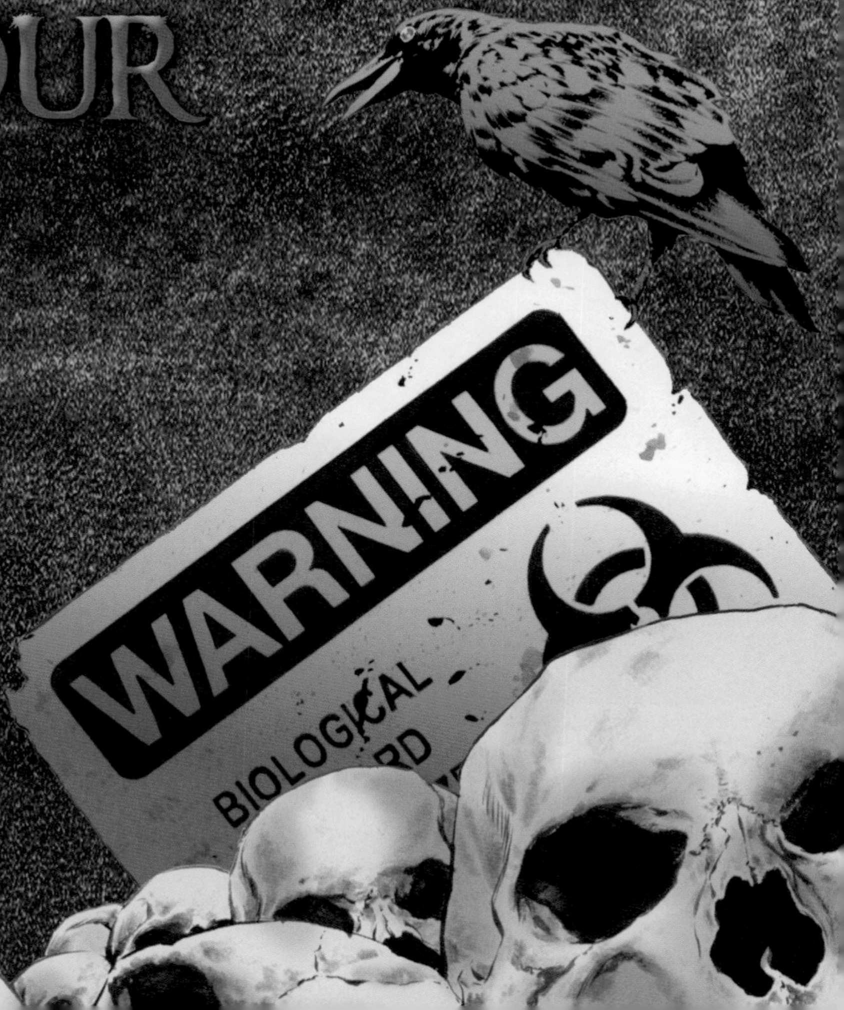
WARNING
BIOLOGICAL

In **one** day, by virtue of a single poster cranked out on a mimeograph machine, the Free Zone had been transformed from a loose group of refugees into potential voters...

The same afternoon the flyers went up, Larry Underwood and Leo Rockway walked west, on Arapahoe Street, towards Harold Lauder's house.

If Larry put his hands in his pockets, Leo did the same. If Larry kicked a can, Leo kicked a stone. When Larry started to whistle, Leo joined him.

For Pete's sake, thought Larry, I'm falling in love with this kid...

At the house Frannie had described:

Harold Lauder, I presume?

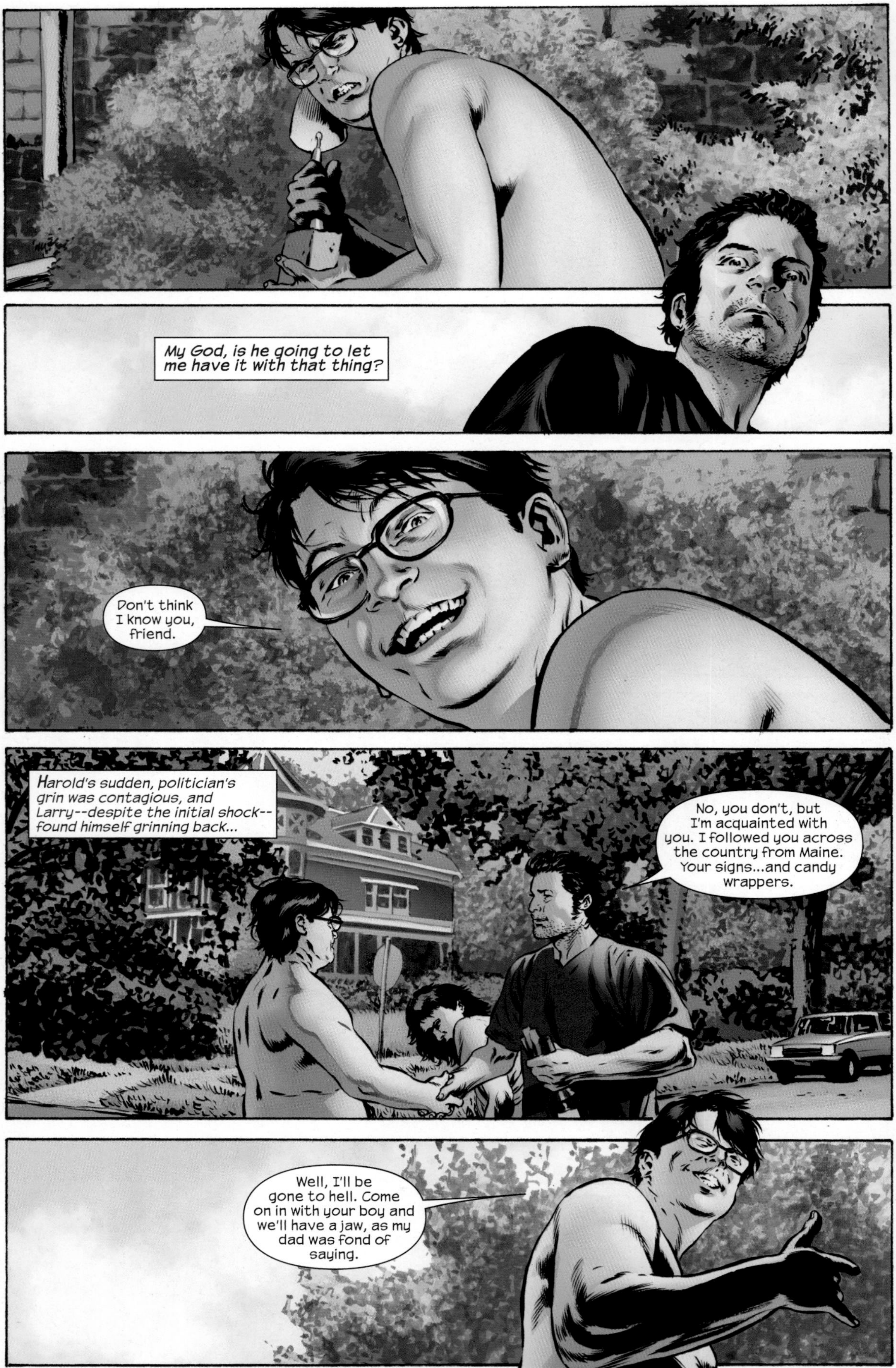

My God, is he going to let me have it with that thing?
Don't think I know you, friend.
Harold's sudden, politician's grin was contagious, and Larry--despite the initial shock--found himself grinning back...
No, you don't, but I'm acquainted with you. I followed you across the country from Maine. Your signs...and candy wrappers.
Well, I'll be gone to hell. Come on in with your boy and we'll have a jaw, as my dad was fond of saying.

In fact, Leo **refused** to go inside with Larry and Harold. He didn't **want** to, he said; he was missing his **Nadine-mom**, he said...

...it's all right. Kids are funny, sometimes.

Well, that one sure is, but I guess he's got a right. He's been through a lot.

I'll pass on the candy bars--I'm off the sweets, trying to lose weight--but we've **got** to have some wine; this is a special occasion.

Have a seat on that green chair; there are some good wine glasses in the basement, I think...

He's just a kid, younger than me, thought Larry, looking around the living room. If he's eighteen, I'll eat the candles on his next birthday ca...

Larry noticed a loose stone on the hearth, looking as if it had come out and then been put back, carelessly...

Larry was **about** to fit the stone back into place when he saw there was a **book** down in the hole, lightly powdered with rockdust:

Wha...?

LEDGER

Feeling ashamed, like he'd been **intentionally** prying, he replaced the rock **just** as Harold's footfalls began to ascend the basement steps.

(Was the book Harold's? Or did it belong to the house's previous owner?)

Upon Harold's return, they cracked open Larry's bottle of Bordeaux. Once they were both pleasantly squiffed:

That big meeting on the eighteenth...

How come you didn't get on that committee, Harold? I would've thought a guy like you would've been a natural.

Well, I'm **awfully** young. Maybe the powers-that-be wanted someone with more... experience.

But who **knows** what lies in the future...?

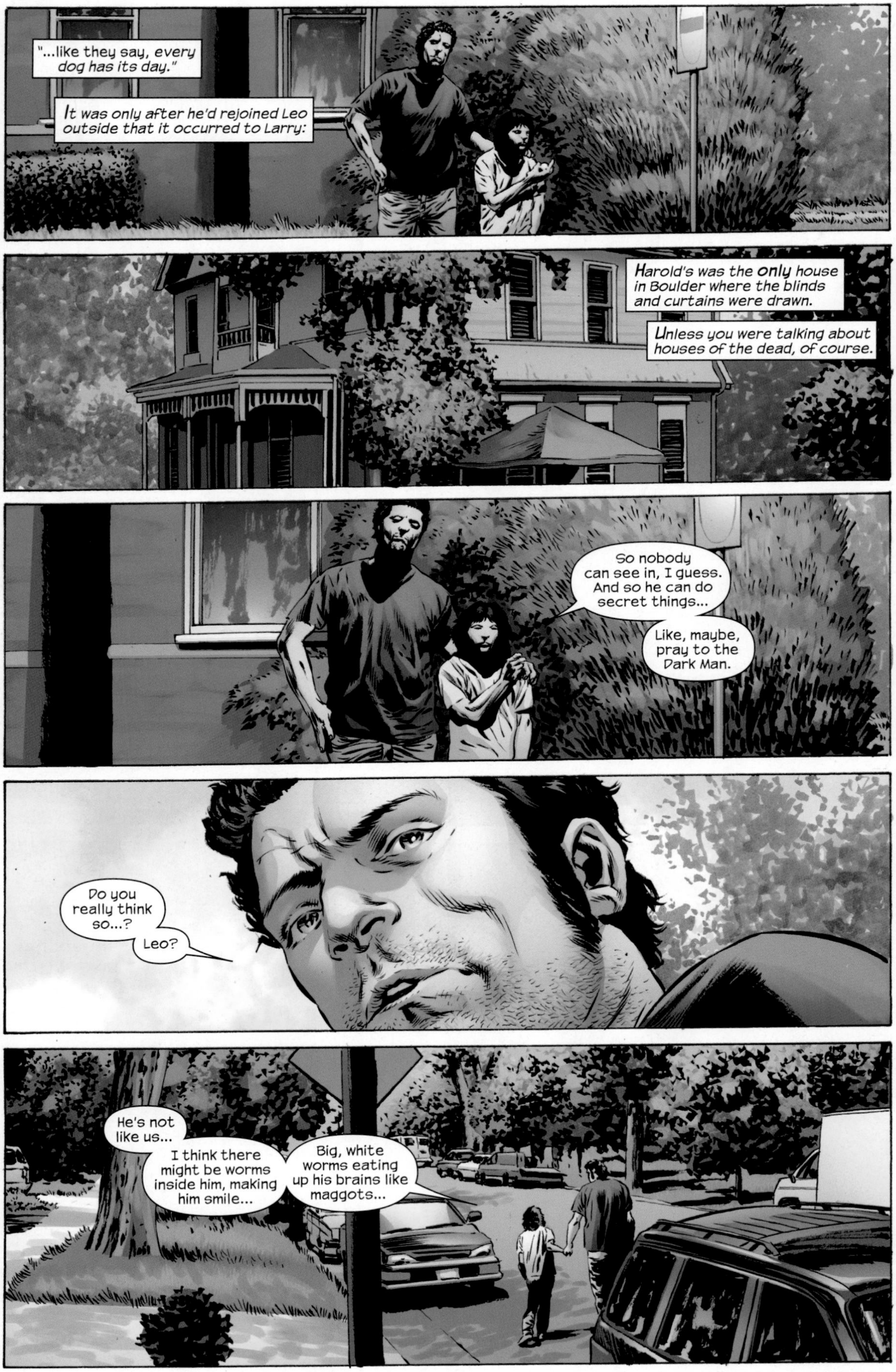
"...like they say, every dog has its day."
It was only after he'd rejoined Leo outside that it occurred to Larry:
Harold's was the only house in Boulder where the blinds and curtains were drawn.
Unless you were talking about houses of the dead, of course.
So nobody can see in, I guess. And so he can do secret things...
Like, maybe, pray to the Dark Man.
Do you really think so...?
Leo?
He's not like us...
I think there might be worms inside him, making him smile...
Big, white worms eating up his brains like maggots...

THE HOUSE ON PEARL AND BROADWAY.
THE BACKYARD.

Stu interrupted Frannie's washing with love-making.

(It hadn't been going well, anyway. Hard as Fran tried, it was *impossible* without a scrub board, and there were none to be found in Boulder.)

Afterwards, they lingered underneath the building's overhang, talking...

Dick wants off the committee. He says until we get a real doctor, he's too busy with the sick.

Just today, he saved a guy who had a gangrenous leg. Dick had to take it off at the knee.

That's awful...

And what, it means we need one more for the committee?

Ralph's gung-ho for this Larry Underwood guy, and from what you say, he struck you as being pretty handy.

He did. And I met his lady, Lucy Swan, in town earlier and she seems sweet.

You gonna go ask him to join?

I want to. But I need to find out what he thought of Harold before asking him along for the ride.

What *is* it about Harold...?

I lied to him once, you know. The day the three of us met. July fourth. I said I didn't want you...

I think he still holds that against me.

I keep *reminding* myself that he's scared and lonely. And probably feeling *rejected* now, since he's not on the ad hoc committee--

That was one of Nick's unilateral decisions.

No one trusts Harold, is the truth. Not with that smile.

In Ogunquit, he was the most insufferable kid... Then, after the flu, he seemed to change... become more of a man...

Then he changed again, all at once... He started to smile all the time and you couldn't really talk to him anymore.

The way people get when they convert to religion or read--

...

Read what? Frannie?

Something that changes their life. Like *Das Kapital* or *Mein Kampf*.

Or maybe just intercepted love letters...

FRAN AND STUART'S BEDROOM.

Of course, there was **no way** to tell if a book had been read, and even if there **were** a way, there would be no way to tell if that person had been Harold Lauder.

*A*nd yet. Frannie sent *Stu* to *Larry's*, then dug out her diary, from the back corner of her closet.

(The way people get when they convert to religion...or read something that changes their lives...like intercepted love letters...)

Heart beating wildly, Frannie began turning through the diary's pages.

There was no reason at all for her to be thinking of the man in black, with his coathanger...but she was.

Sentences jumped out at her, shutterclicks of the recent past that *slapped* her.

Harold will object on principles, of course. Damn you, Harold, grow up!

Well, you know Harold, all those pompous words...an insecure little boy...

Harold's breath would have driven a dragon away tonight...

Harold stores up rebuffs like pirate treasure...

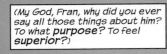

(My God, Fran, why did you ever say all those things about him? To what *purpose*? To feel *superior*?)

Then, on August 1, two weeks ago: No entry last night, I was too happy. Have I ever been this happy? I don't think so. Stu and I are together. We--

Frannie turned the page to read the rest of the entry:

--made love twice.

But the words *barely* caught her eye.

Her glance dropped halfway down the page, to something that froze her solid...

A dark, smeary fingerprint.

Much larger than *her* thumb, and not grease or oil, but dried chocolate...

Harold and his candybars.

For a moment, she was afraid to turn around--afraid she might see Harold grinning like the *Cheshire Cat: Every dog has its day, Frannie.*

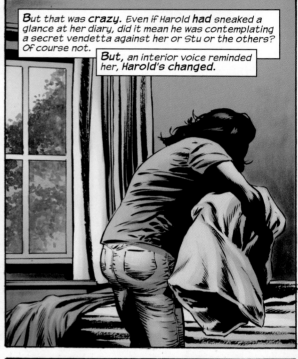

But that was *crazy.* Even if Harold *had* sneaked a glance at her diary, did it mean he was contemplating a secret vendetta against her or Stu or the others? Of course not.

But, an interior voice reminded her, *Harold's changed.*

Goddamnit, he hasn't changed *that* much!

Frannie *flinched* a little at the sound of her own voice in the empty room...

...then went downstairs to get supper started.

She and Stu were eating early--as soon as Stu got back from Larry's--because of the meeting...

...which suddenly didn't seem as *important* as it had earlier.

There's a boy, Leo Rockaway, that came across from Maine with us, who kind of *sees* into people... When I went to visit Harold, Leo wouldn't go into Harold's house. Wouldn't even stay on his lawn.

After meeting Harold, even though we had a good time, I sort of understood *why* Leo didn't want to...

Yeah, that's Harold for you... Listen, Larry, I came to ask if you'd serve on our little ad hoc committee. We need one more, and you come highly recommended.

What do you say? Wanna ride along?

I thought nothing in the world would make me happier than to get here and dump my people and let somebody *else* take over for a change. Instead, I've been just about bored out of my head...

Oh, hell, I say yes.

We're having a little pow-wow at my place tonight to talk over the big meeting on the eighteenth. Think you can come?

Sure. Can I bring my gal, Lucy?

'Fraid not. Nor talk to her about it. We want to keep some of this stuff close for a while.

I'm not much on cloak-and-dagger stuff, Stu...

I agree with you, Larry, but this is *wartime*.

That man we all dreamed about... None of us think he's gone away. And though most of the people here may not be thinking about him, I'd bet my bottom dollar he's thinking about us.

You think that lunatic's after us...

That's a nice thought to have just before dinner.

Larry, I'm not sure of *anything*. But Mother Abagail says it won't be over, one way or the other, until he's got us or we've got him.

...

Point taken. We talk it out and keep our mouths shut.

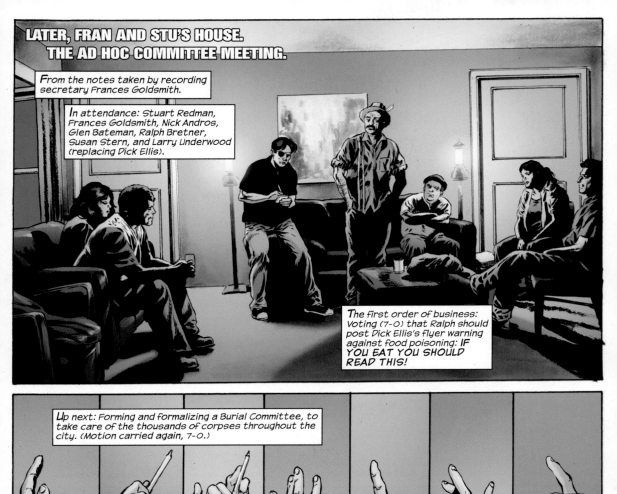

From the notes taken by recording secretary Frances Goldsmith.

In attendance: Stuart Redman, Frances Goldsmith, Nick Andros, Glen Bateman, Ralph Bretner, Susan Stern, and Larry Underwood (replacing Dick Ellis).

The first order of business: Voting (7-0) that Ralph should post Dick Ellis's flyer warning against food poisoning: IF YOU EAT YOU SHOULD READ THIS!

Up next: Forming and formalizing a Burial Committee, to take care of the thousands of corpses throughout the city. (Motion carried again, 7-0.)

Then Nick Andros was recognized, and he related (through Ralph) a discussion he'd had with Mother Abagail earlier.

He explained how she believes that all of the survivors are part of a chess game between God and Satan, and that Satan's chief agent in this game is the Adversary, Randall Flagg.

Also, that **she** believes **she** is God's chief agent.

And that she wants, whenever the committee's deliberations touch on the Dark Man or the struggle, to be informed and consulted.

In this vein, Nick introduced a series of motions:

THE COMMITTEE SHOULD NOT DISCUSS THE RELIGIOUS AND/OR SUPERNATURAL IMPLICATIONS OF THE 'ADVERSARY' DURING MEETINGS, BUT THAT WE TREAT HIM AS REAL, A REAL THREAT

THE MAIN, SECRET BUSINESS OF THE COMMITTEE BE HOW TO DEAL WITH THE 'ADVERSARY', AKA RANDALL FLAGG.

MOTHER ABAGAIL TO BE KEPT INFORMED OF ALL BUSINESS TRANSACTED BY THE COMMITTEE.

Motions passed, 7-0.

Then Nick suggested we send three volunteers to join the dark man's people, the purpose being to gain intelligence about the goings-on in Vegas.

I'll do it, I'll go.

That's honorable, Susan, but the fact is, we don't know if the people we send will ever come back, or when, or in what shape...

In the meantime, this committee has the not inconsiderable job of getting things up and running in Boulder...

After some hot discussion, it was resolved, gloomily, that no one from the ad hoc committee be eligible to volunteer for this reconnaissance.

I just hate the idea of us sending *other people* over there, maybe to be crucified on a telephone pole...

We may not like it, but we're politicians here. And this is the life-and-death of everyone in Boulder...

I never thought I'd be a politician.

Join the club.

Larry Underwood put forth a potential emissary: Judge Farris.

He's the sharpest old guy I've met, and for the record, he's only 70.

Lively discussion followed, but it was decided that the advantages of sending the Judge outweighed the disadvantages.

Committee voted aye to asking Judge Farris, 7-0.

I went along with yours, Larry, maybe you'll go along with my idea: Dayna Jurgens. She's got more guts than any woman I know.

With almost no discussion, Committee voted aye, 7-0.

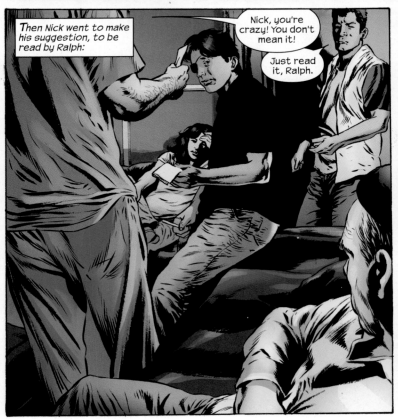

Then Nick went to make his suggestion, to be read by Ralph:

Nick, you're crazy! You don't mean it!

Just read it, Ralph.

...

Well, it says here he wants to nominate... Tom Cullen.

Uproar from the Committee, but Nick argued the same point Larry had about the Judge:

That just as the Adversary wouldn't expect us to send an old man to spy, nor would he expect a retarded person.

That if Tom were given a simple story and told he **had** to stick to it, Tom **would**, whatever torture might be inflicted upon him.

It wouldn't come to *that*, would it? Nobody *really* believes it would come to--

Nick has the floor, Frannie, let him finish.

Nick did, by explaining that Tom could be given a post-hypnotic suggestion before being sent out--to return after a certain amount of time. The full moon, say.

(Nick had already tested hypnotizing Tom, with help from a gentleman named Stan Nogotny; it worked like gangbusters.)

Originally, Nick had the idea because he thought Tom, himself, practiced a kind of *self*-hypnosis, whenever Tom "vanished within himself" to make sense of something.

Nick's last point was that by putting Tom into deep hypnosis upon his return from Vegas, he would have almost perfect recall of everything he saw.

It sounds like that old movie *The Manchurian Candidate* to me...

*Before we voted on Tom, I had **my** say:*

Do we **really** want to take that sweet, **foggy** boy and turn him into a human U-2 plane? What do we do if they kill him, Nick? If they kill any of the people we send? Breed up a new, **improved** version of Captain Trips?

WHAT FRAN BRINGS UP AFFECTS ME DEEPLY, BUT WE'RE DOING ALL OF THIS FOR MOTHER ABAGAIL AND HER IDEAS...

...ALSO, I KNOW THIS BEING — FLAGG — IS EVIL...

IF ANYONE WORKS UP A NEW STRAIN OF SUPERFLU, IT WILL BE HIM TO USE ON US, AND I'D LIKE TO STOP HIM WHILE WE STILL CAN...

But we're putting our hand on the same switch as Flagg to stop him...

Once it's all over...even if we win...will we be able to **let go** of the switch?

Let's...

...let's go around the table.

I vote aye.

AYE.

I don't like it much, either, but if Nick's going for it, aye.

Nay.

Aye.

Nay.

I think the idea stinks like a pay toilet, but this is the kind of stuff you get when you're at the top, I guess. Aye.

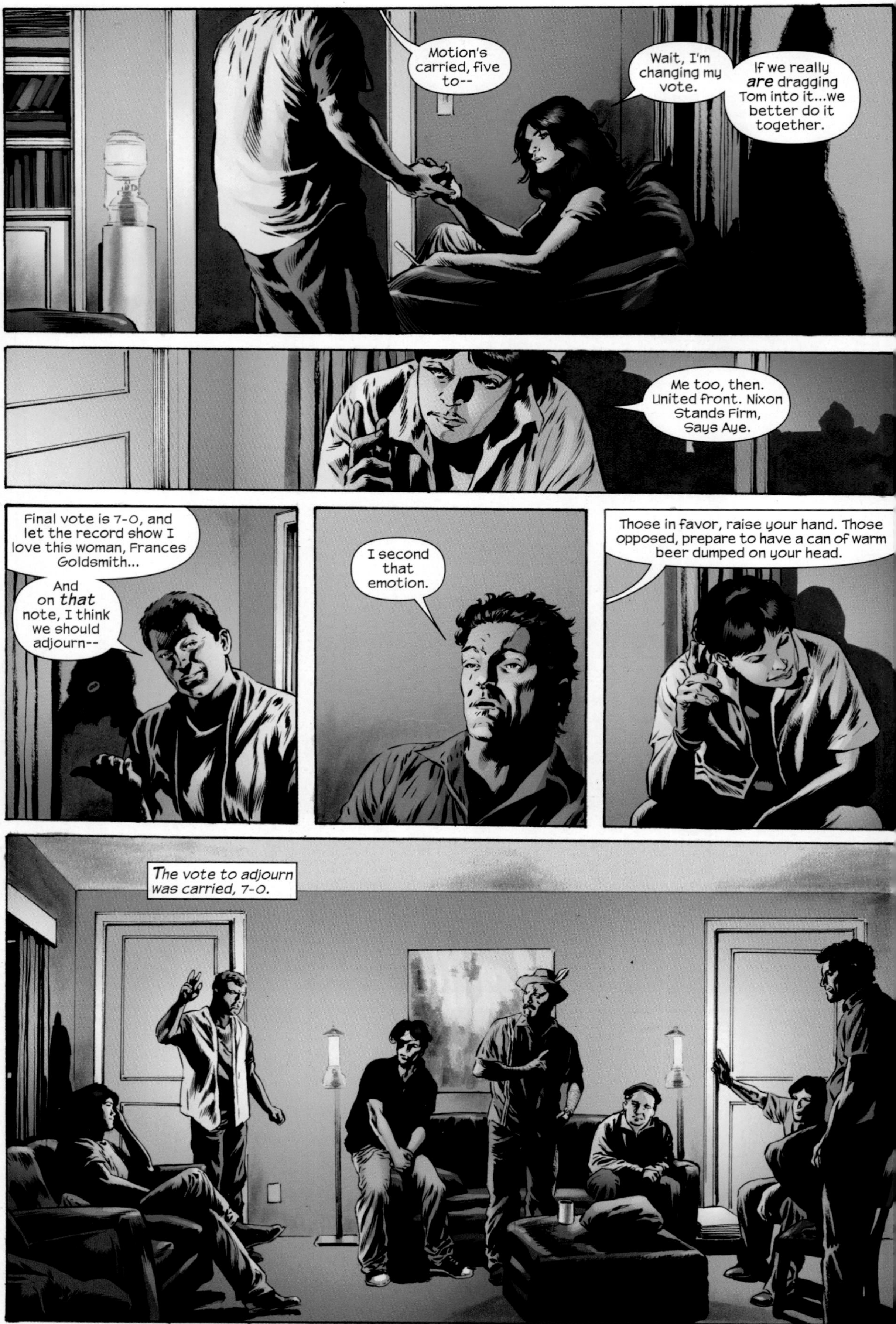

Motion's carried, five to--
Wait, I'm changing my vote.
If we really *are* dragging Tom into it...we better do it together.
Me too, then. United front. Nixon Stands Firm, Says Aye.
Final vote is 7-0, and let the record show I love this woman, Frances Goldsmith...
And on *that* note, I think we should adjourn--
I second that emotion.
Those in favor, raise your hand. Those opposed, prepare to have a can of warm beer dumped on your head.
The vote to adjourn was carried, 7-0.

Coming to bed, Stu?

Yeah, I was just...

You were right, Frannie. It's a dirty business, sending out spies. Only trouble is... Nick was right, too. In a case like this, what do you do?

Vote your conscience and then get the best night sleep you can, I guess.

... I love you, Fran.

She almost said something then. Not about Tom Cullen; she'd made her peace with that...

...but Harold's smudged chocolate thumbprint was still on her mind.

(Every dog has its day, Fran.)

In the end, Fran didn't mention it. If there was a problem, it was her problem. She would just have to wait...watch...and see if anything happened.

It was a long time before she slept.

In the early hours of the morning, Mother Abagail was praying:

Show me my sin, Lord. I know I missed something you wanted me to see... I can't sleep, I can't take a crap, I don't *feel* you, Lord... How have I offended Thee?

She listened for the small, still voice in her heart, but all was silent and dark there.

Please my God, my God, please my--

Not God, old woman. Me.

I'm coming for you, Mother...We'll run you like dogs run deer...I am all the things you think I am, but more. I'm the magic man, the man who speaks for the latter age... Your own people know me best, Mother. They call me John the Conqueror...

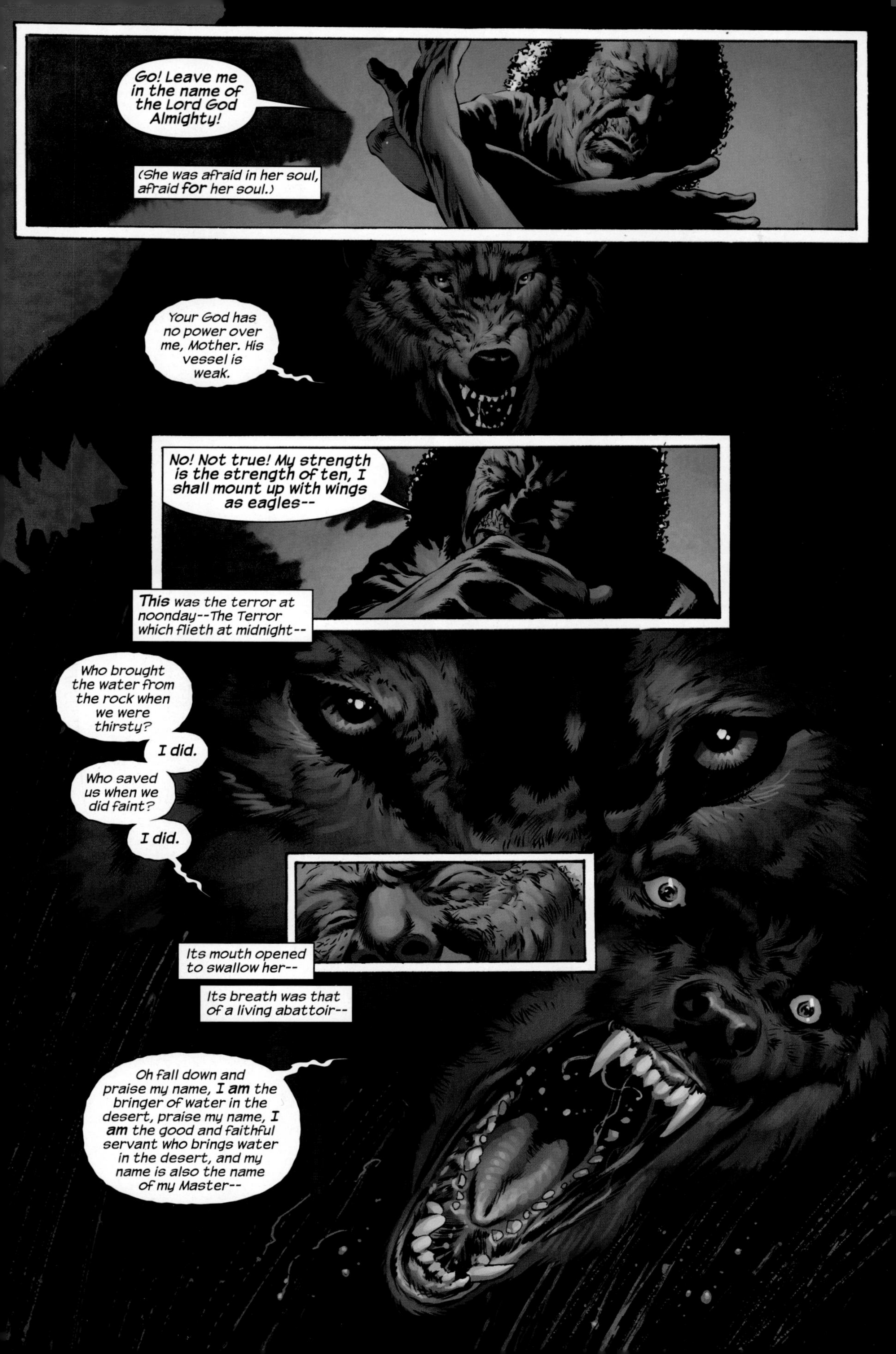
Go! Leave me in the name of the Lord God Almighty!
(She was afraid in her soul, afraid for her soul.)
Your God has no power over me, Mother. His vessel is weak.
No! Not true! My strength is the strength of ten, I shall mount up with wings as eagles--
This was the terror at noonday--The Terror which flieth at midnight--
Who brought the water from the rock when we were thirsty?
I did.
Who saved us when we did faint?
I did.
Its mouth opened to swallow her--
Its breath was that of a living abattoir--
Oh fall down and praise my name, I am the bringer of water in the desert, praise my name, I am the good and faithful servant who brings water in the desert, and my name is also the name of my Master--

...my name...

...praise my name, praise God from whom all blessings flow, praise Him ye creatures here below...

Her Bible had fallen to the floor. There was dawnlight in the window.

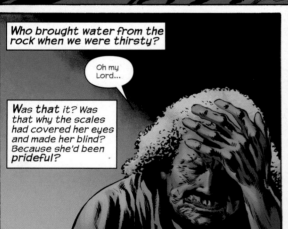

Who brought water from the rock when we were thirsty?

Oh my Lord...

Was that it? Was that why the scales had covered her eyes and made her blind? Because she'd been prideful?

Bitter tears began to roll down her cheeks as she climbed, slowly and painfully, to her arthritic feet...

She turned to look out the window and knew what she had to do...

Thy will be done.

An hour later, Abagail was walking slowly west on Mapleton Avenue, toward the wooded tangles and narrow-throated defiles beyond town, leaving Boulder behind her.

chapter FIVE

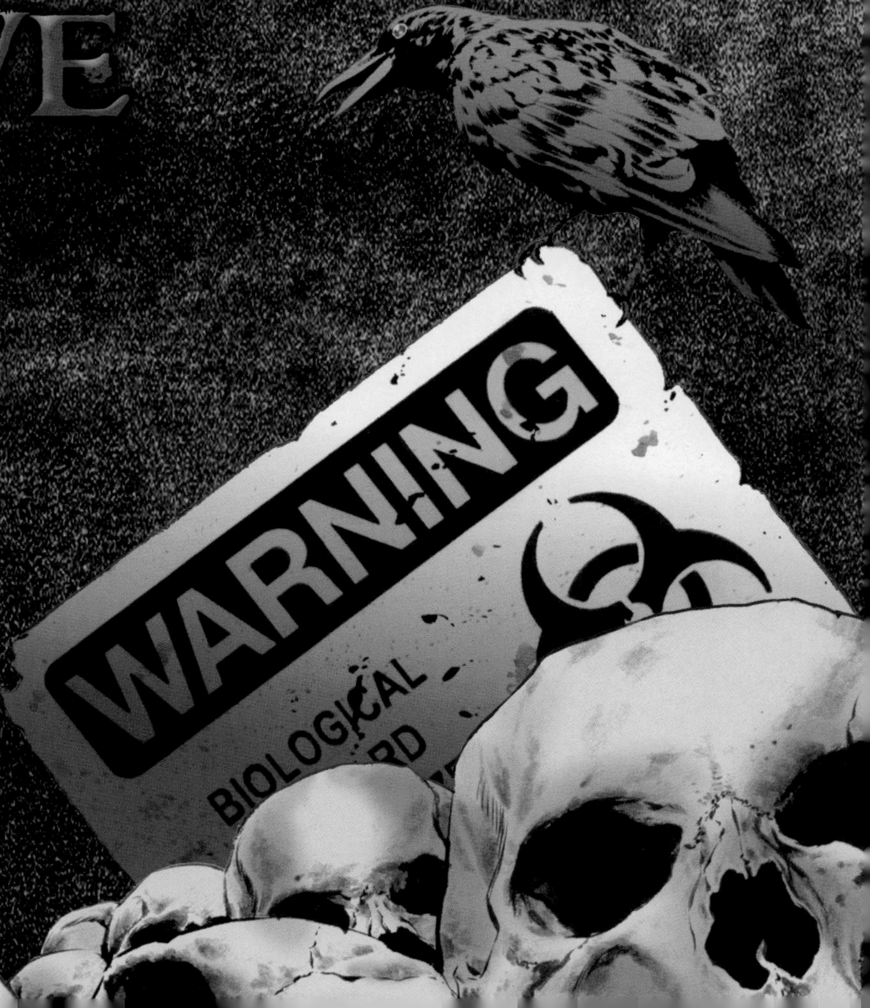
WARNING
BIOLOGICAL

By noon, news of Mother Abagail's disappearance--days before the Free Zone's first, all-important Town Hall Meeting--swept Boulder.

The community's collective sense was that she must've gone off to "pray for guidance." The general mood was more of unhappy resignation than alarm...

I must be gone a bit now. I've sinned and presumed to know the mind of God. My sin has been PRIDE, and HE wants me to find my place in His work again. I will be with you again if it is God's will. Abby Freemantl

...except at the Power Plant, where efforts to get the juice flowing again were interrupted by Glen's arrival with Mother Abagail's note.

We can't let an old woman wander the frigging wilderness like some Old Testament guy until she dies of exposure!

Slow down, Stu. Let's try to look at the implications of this.

If the Pope decides he has to walk to Jerusalem, do you argue with him if you're a good Catholic?

To hell with the implications, Glen!

It's *not* the same thing and you know it!

It showers just about every afternoon... If she gets soaked, Mother's sure to take a cold. Then what? Pneumonia? At her age?

Ralph's right; we have to--

We *have* to pull together a search party--

How far could she have gotten?

EVEN IF YOU FOUND HER, HOW WOULD YOU BRING HER BACK? CHAINS?

Of course not! But we can't do *nothing*!

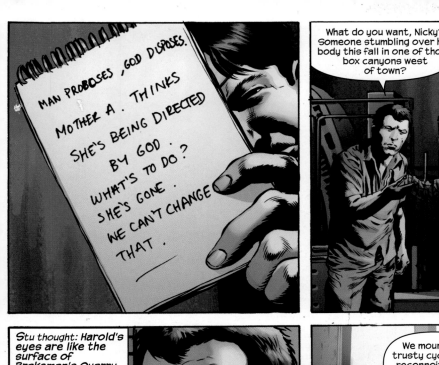

MAN PROPOSES, GOD DISPOSES.

MOTHER A. THINKS SHE'S BEING DIRECTED BY GOD. WHAT'S TO DO? SHE'S GONE. WE CAN'T CHANGE THAT.

What do you want, Nicky? Someone stumbling over her body this fall in one of those box canyons west of town?

It was her decision to go, Stu, we have to honor that.

I have an idea.

Stu thought: *Harold's eyes are like the surface of Brakeman's Quarry back home.*

The water looked pleasant enough, but four boys had drowned in its black depths over the years...

What's...

...what's your notion, Harold?

We mount our trusty cycles and reconnoiter the area west of Boulder.

If we find her, we don't *force* her to do anything, but we can at least keep tabs on her. Ask if she wants or needs anything.

Like a ride back to town.

...

I think it's a helluva good idea, Harold. If there are no objections...

"...I'll just swing by home and leave a note for Fran."

She'd been at the library in downtown Boulder, reading up on gardening, when she heard about Mother Abagail taking her leave.

Fran went straight to the apartment, missing Stu and the others by a few minutes. His note was short:

BACK BY 9:30. I'M WITH RALPH + HAROLD.

Immediately, she worried. A man who would steal your diary (Harold!) and pilfer your thoughts might creep up behind someone he hated (Stu!) and give him a push off a high place. Or use a rock. Or a knife. Or a gun.

So Harold's house on Arapahoe might be deserted until nine-thirty tonight...

Three minutes later, biking up Broadway, Frannie was wondering what she would do if she actually found something incriminating at Harold's...

The truth was, she had no idea.

The house was deserted and locked, except for a cellar window through which Frannie wriggled.

Why do you lock your doors, Harold, when everything's free? Because nobody is as afraid of robbery as a thief?

The basement had been finished into the kind of rumpus room her dad had always talked about but never gotten around to doing.

With that thought came a sudden wave of homesickness for Ogunquit, for the ocean, for the good old Maine hills and pines...

If you have to have a cry, Frannie old kid old sock, have it later, not here in Harold Lauder's house.

Business first.

Upstairs, the living room's nicest feature was a fireplace, with a stone hearth wide enough to sit on.

Which Frannie did, looking around thoughtfully.

As she shifted, she felt a loose hearthstone under her fanny.

KNOCK,
KNOCK,
KNOCK.

My God, Fran thought, *The shades are down, at least. And my bike is in the backyard, out of sight--*

Hello? Anyone home?

The knob of the front door began to turn in frustrated half-circles...

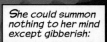

She could summon nothing to her mind except gibberish:

Before removing the mote from thy neighbor's eye, remove the pie from thine own...

Then, after an *excruciating* few moments, and with an indescribable sense of relief, she heard footfalls clicking away from the house, down Harold's concrete path.

Fran ran down the hall to peek out. She *had* to see...

The Cross woman, the one who came over with Larry Underwood, she thought. Does she know Harold?

Five minutes later, too nervous to search any further, she boosted herself back through the cellar window on a wicker chair she had pulled over, then moved back to its original position.

Once home, she concluded, simply, that she was not one for housebreaking.

Oh, Stu, I need you...

Please come home...

Harold had asked for Nederland because it was the least likely area to find anything.

He didn't think *he* could walk from Boulder to Nederland in one day, let alone that crazy old bag.

¿...Sunrise Amphitheater... No sign of her... storm's coming up over here...?

Ralph was way up on Flagstaff Mountain, but Stu was in Chautauqua Park, only about four miles from Harold.

Ten-four, Ralph, you there? Calling Harold Lauder. You copy, Harold?

I'm here. I was off to the side... Thought I saw something in a ditch, but it was just an old jacket, over.

Yeah, okay. Why don't you come down to Chautauqua, Harold, and we'll wait for Ralph together, copy?

You like giving orders, don't you, suckhole? I might have something for you. Yes, I just might.

Sorry, Stu, I was woolgathering. I can be there in fifteen minutes. Over and out.

Harold took a moment. He felt he was at a point of balance...about to shift.

He was wearing an army surplus flak jacket for the mountain chill, but also because it hid the Smith & Wesson .38 in one of its zippered pockets.

He'd initiated this expedition on the chance that he might be alone with Stu long enough to actually do it...

Tonight?

Why not?

On his way to Nederland, Harold had felt a stupendous, irrational power coming from the West, so great that he worried it might drive him mad.

He felt that, if he ventured much further towards Vegas, self-will would be lost. He would go just as he was, empty-handed...

...and for that, although he could not be blamed, the dark man would kill him.

It was ten to seven, now. He could waste both Redman and Bretner by 7:30; Fran wouldn't raise the alarm until 10:30; by then, he would be well on his way to Nevada...

Smiling, Harold Lauder drove towards Chautauqua Park.

Nothing, huh? Never mind, it was a good idea. For all we know, she's back at her house right now. If not, we can look again tomorrow, before the meeting.

Hopefully we won't be looking for a body.

Hopefully not...

Listen, Harold, why don't you come back to supper with me?

What?

Supper.

Frannie'd be glad to see you, too. She really would.

...

I...

...I had a thing for her, you know. Maybe it's best if we just...let it go for now. Nothing personal. Just... the two of you belong together, I know that.

Your choice, Harold, but the door's open anytime.

And thank you, for pushing that we look for Mother, even if it came to nothing.

Will you shake with me?

Harold stared at Stu blankly for a moment...

...then took his right hand out of his jacket pocket--it seemed to catch on something, maybe the zipper--and shook Stu's hand.

Glen Bateman joined them a few moments later.

Harold slipped away from them, as quickly as possible, his face strained and white, his voice oddly flat.

Stu thought it must've been his disappointment that they hadn't found Mother Abagail affecting him.

When he got home, Harold was on the verge of tears and shaking so bad he could barely get his key in the front door.

He wrote in his ledger for nearly an hour and a half, until it was all out of him—his terror and his fury and his frustration—and his resolve was strong again.

After putting his ledger away, Harold thought, calmly, how **close** he had come to mowing Stu down with his .38.

That would have put the other members of their sanctimonious ad hoc committee in a mood for their meeting.

But there would be other chances. After all, the mark of genius is its ability to abide. And so he would—

Harold froze.

The basement door was standing open.

He kept it closed tight, always.

Who's there?

In the basement, Harold saw something on the floor, beneath the windows.

A spill of brown grit. And in the grit, as clear as a fingerprint...

...the track of a sneaker or tennis shoe.

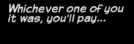

You'll pay...

Whichever one of you it was, you'll pay...

But Harold had an idea who it was...

He'd have to come up with a better hiding place for his ledger, he knew that. It was a dangerous book, and if someone found it, it was over.

He kept thinking of Fran's shoes... (Patterns of soles, patterns of souls...)

When Harold finally did sleep, he cried out miserably in his dreams, as if to ward off things that had already been let in forever.

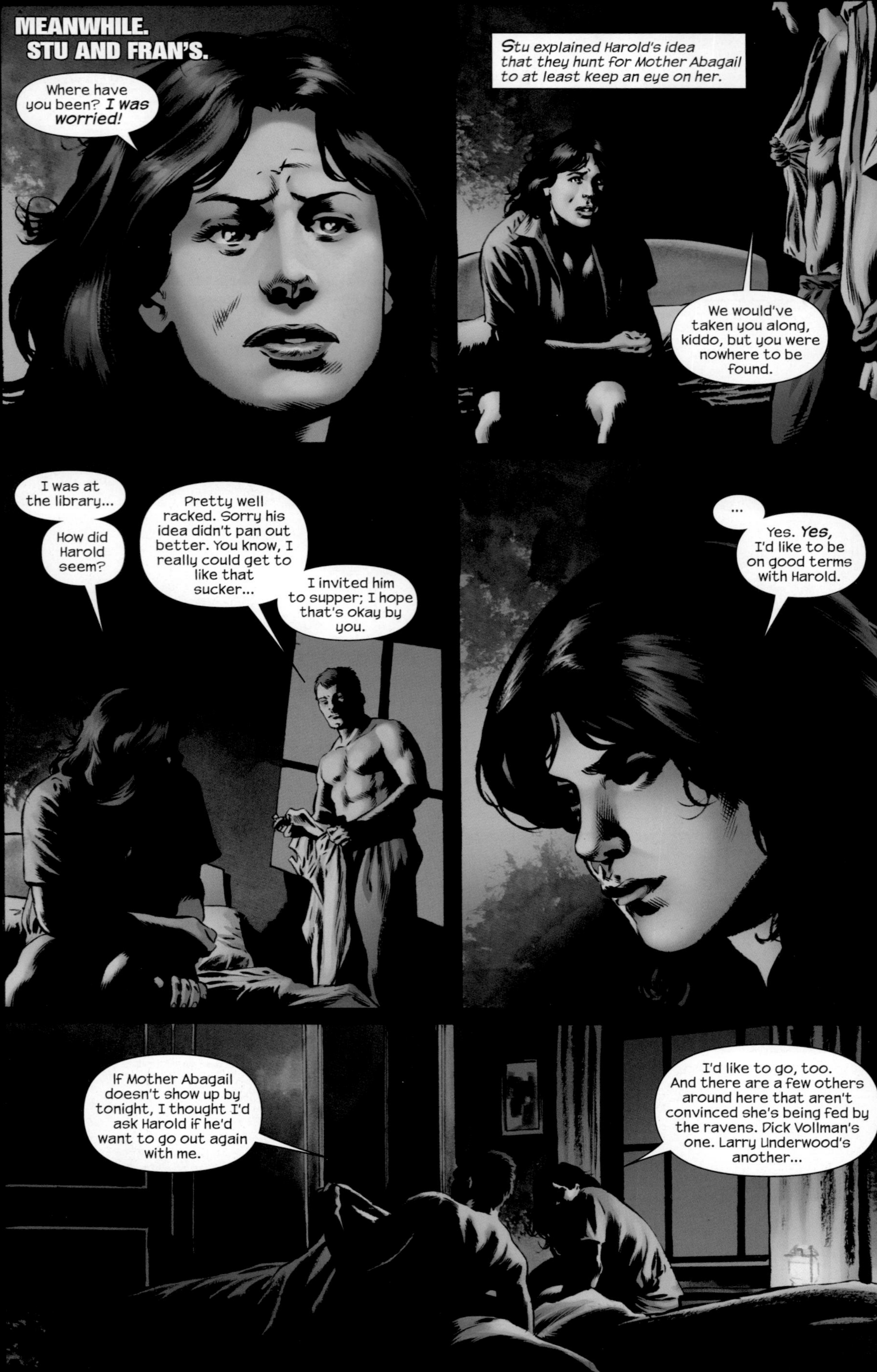

MEANWHILE. STU AND FRAN'S.
Where have you been? I was worried!
Stu explained Harold's idea that they hunt for Mother Abagail to at least keep an eye on her.
We would've taken you along, kiddo, but you were nowhere to be found.
I was at the library...
How did Harold seem?
Pretty well racked. Sorry his idea didn't pan out better. You know, I really could get to like that sucker...
I invited him to supper; I hope that's okay by you.
...
Yes. Yes, I'd like to be on good terms with Harold.
If Mother Abagail doesn't show up by tonight, I thought I'd ask Harold if he'd want to go out again with me.
I'd like to go, too. And there are a few others around here that aren't convinced she's being fed by the ravens. Dick Vollman's one. Larry Underwood's another...

The search-party started out modestly with half-a-dozen folks, but by dusk, there were better than fifty people combing the brush west of Boulder.

The Free Zone's mood had shifted to dread. Despite the powerful dreams that accorded Mother Abagail a semidivine status, most people were still realists. The woman was well over a hundred years old, and she had been out a night all on her own...

...and now, a second night was coming on.

By dusk, a breeze from the mountains was throwing a splatter of rain against the windows of Fran and Stu's apartment. They were both feeling low and unhappy--

--when Glen burst in.

Stu--
Fran--
Oh, man, I'm glad you're here.

What's wrong, Glen? Is it...?

Did someone find her?

No. It's not bad news, it's good news.

But it's strange...

You...you better come over to my place.

I came home from looking and he was on the porch, fast asleep...

He's really scrawny, and he's been fighting, but it's Kojak...

I'll be... Say, that's a good boy. Good dog, Kojak.

He *followed* me... That's the kind of thing you read about in Star Weekly... Faithful Dog Follows Master Two Thousand Miles... How could he have gotten here?

Maybe...

Maybe the same way we did.

Are you saying--?

Dogs *do* dream, you know.

Is *that* what happened with you, boy?

...did *you* dream about Mother, too?

In fact, Kojak (who still thought of himself occasionally as *Big Steve*, which had been his original name) followed the scent of *The Man* all the way to Hemmingford Home...

...where *four* wolves came out of the corn like ragged spirits of the dead and set upon him.

The fight had been brutal.

(Indeed, even when Kojak was an old, old dog--and he would live another sixteen years, long after Glen Bateman died--the wounds he received in that battle would ache and throb on wet days.)

Kojak killed two of the wolves and sent the other two scurrying away...

...before crawling under the porch to hide from an unseen thing that felt like a *Man* and a *Wolf* and an *Eye*, a *dark thing* like an ancient crocodile in the corn...

Some unknown time later, Kojak emerged from beneath the porch, sure of where to go.

And it was not *The Man's* scent guiding him, it was a *Dream* to the west of him. Of him chasing rabbits through clover that was wet with soothing dew...

CHAUTAUQUA AUDITORIUM.
THE FIRST FREE ZONE TOWN MEETING.

The turnout was almost *total*, and for the first time, Larry Underwood got an idea of how *large* the community was becoming in Boulder.

It all came down to this. Mother Abagail would've endorsed all seven members of the ad hoc committee in one fell swoop, but now, each one of them would have to be nominated and seconded separately.

Larry's hands were damp and chilly; in his heart, he heard his mother's voice: **There's something left out of you, Lar--**

You'll be fine.

Huh? Lucy?

Don't be nervous, Larry.

Stu began the meeting by introducing each member of the ad hoc committee--

--one by one.

When it was Larry's turn to stand, he thought:

Once, in another world, there would have been concerts, and this kind of applause would have been reserved for "Baby, Can You Dig Your Man?"

This wasn't on the agenda, but I wonder if we couldn't start by singing the National Anthem. I guess you folks remember the words and the tune.

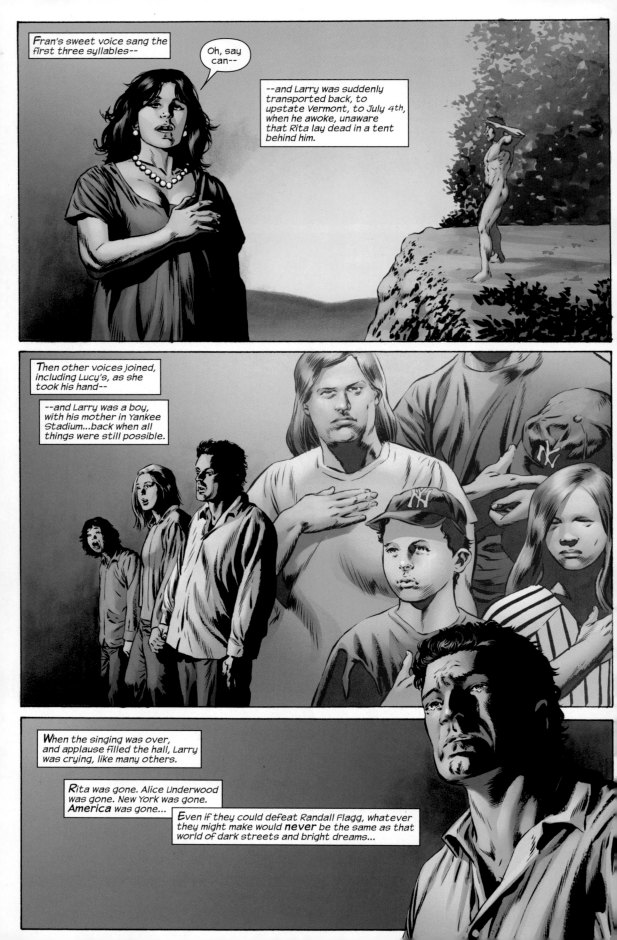

Fran's sweet voice sang the first three syllables--

Oh, say can--

--and Larry was suddenly transported back, to upstate Vermont, to July 4th, when he awoke, unaware that Rita lay dead in a tent behind him.

Then other voices joined, including Lucy's, as she took his hand--

--and Larry was a boy, with his mother in Yankee Stadium...back when all things were still possible.

When the singing was over, and applause filled the hall, Larry was crying, like many others.

Rita was gone. Alice Underwood was gone. New York was gone. *America* was gone...

Even if they could defeat Randall Flagg, whatever they might make would *never* be the same as that world of dark streets and bright dreams...

The meeting continued.

Stu asked that the Free Zone citizens accept both the Constitution and the Bill of Rights as governing law. A voice in the back seconded the motion, so:

Those in favor say aye.

"Aye," to the rooftops.

They like to vote, thought Stu. Good.

Now we see if this is gonna go easy or hard.

The next item on the agenda reads, "To see if the Free Zone will nominate and elect a slate of seven Free Zone representatives."

That means--

Mr. Chairman? Mr. Chairman!

Harold Lauder...

Nick had blocked Harold from serving on the ad hoc committee... Was this his moment of revenge?

Was he about to accuse them of a railroad job? (Which, in a way, is what they were committing?)

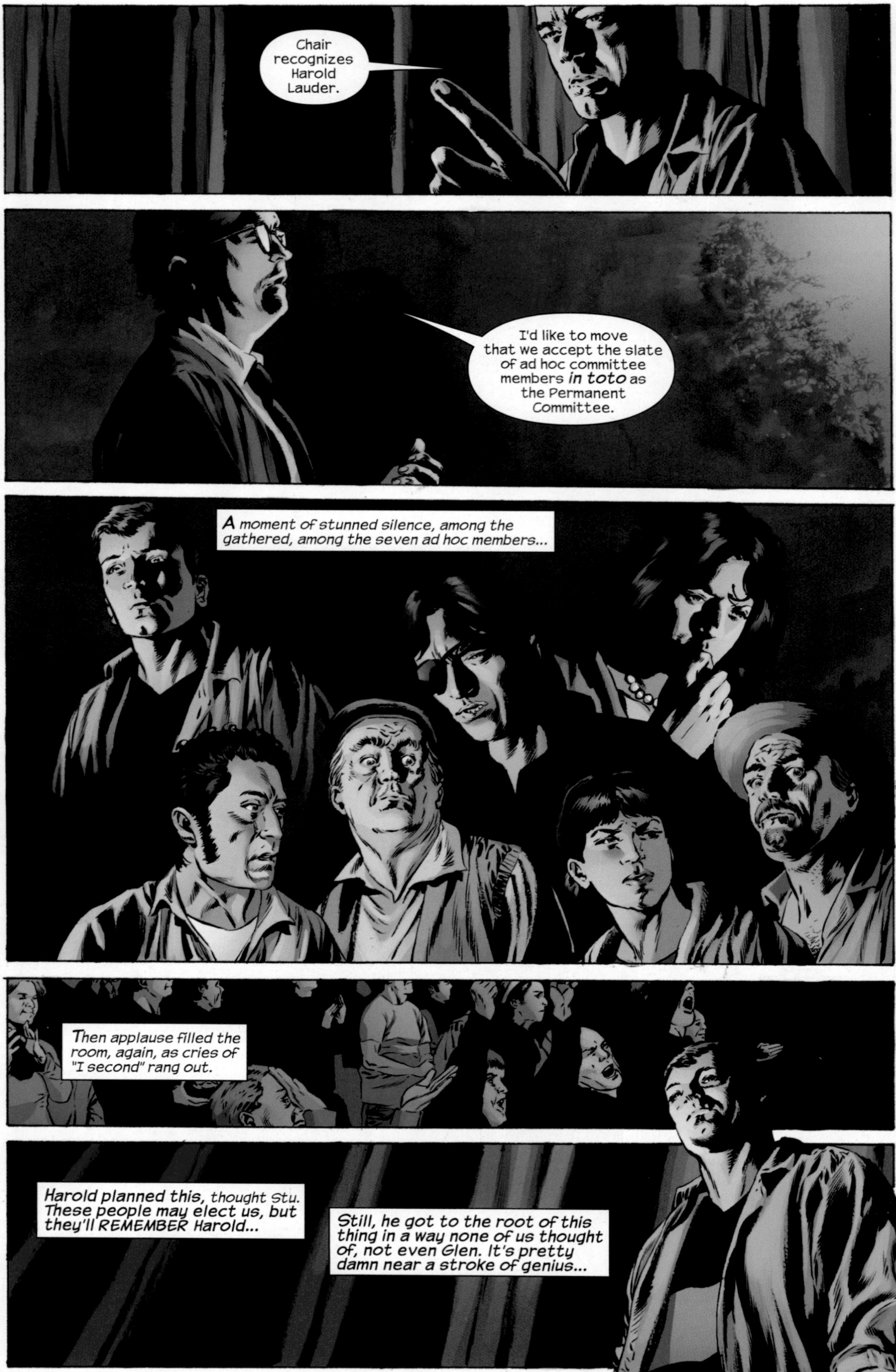
Chair recognizes Harold Lauder.
I'd like to move that we accept the slate of ad hoc committee members in toto as the Permanent Committee.
A moment of stunned silence, among the gathered, among the seven ad hoc members...
Then applause filled the room, again, as cries of "I second" rang out.
Harold planned this, thought Stu. These people may elect us, but they'll REMEMBER Harold...
Still, he got to the root of this thing in a way none of us thought of, not even Glen. It's pretty damn near a stroke of genius...

Let's vote, then. Those in favor of Harold Lauder's motion that we accept the ad hoc committee just as it stands as the Permanent Free Zone Committee, please signify by saying aye.

"Aye," they bellowed, sending the barnswallows above them into a frenzy.

Opposed?

There was not a single "nay" in the chamber...

...so Stu pushed on to the next item on the agenda, feeling *slightly* dazed.

As if someone--namely, Harold Lauder--had crept up behind him and clopped him on the head with a large sledgehammer made out of Silly Putty.

Stu wondered, suddenly, if he had been wrong about Harold turning over a new leaf. He worried, dimly, that this was the first move of a confidence game Harold was playing with them.

Well, they would find out soon enough.

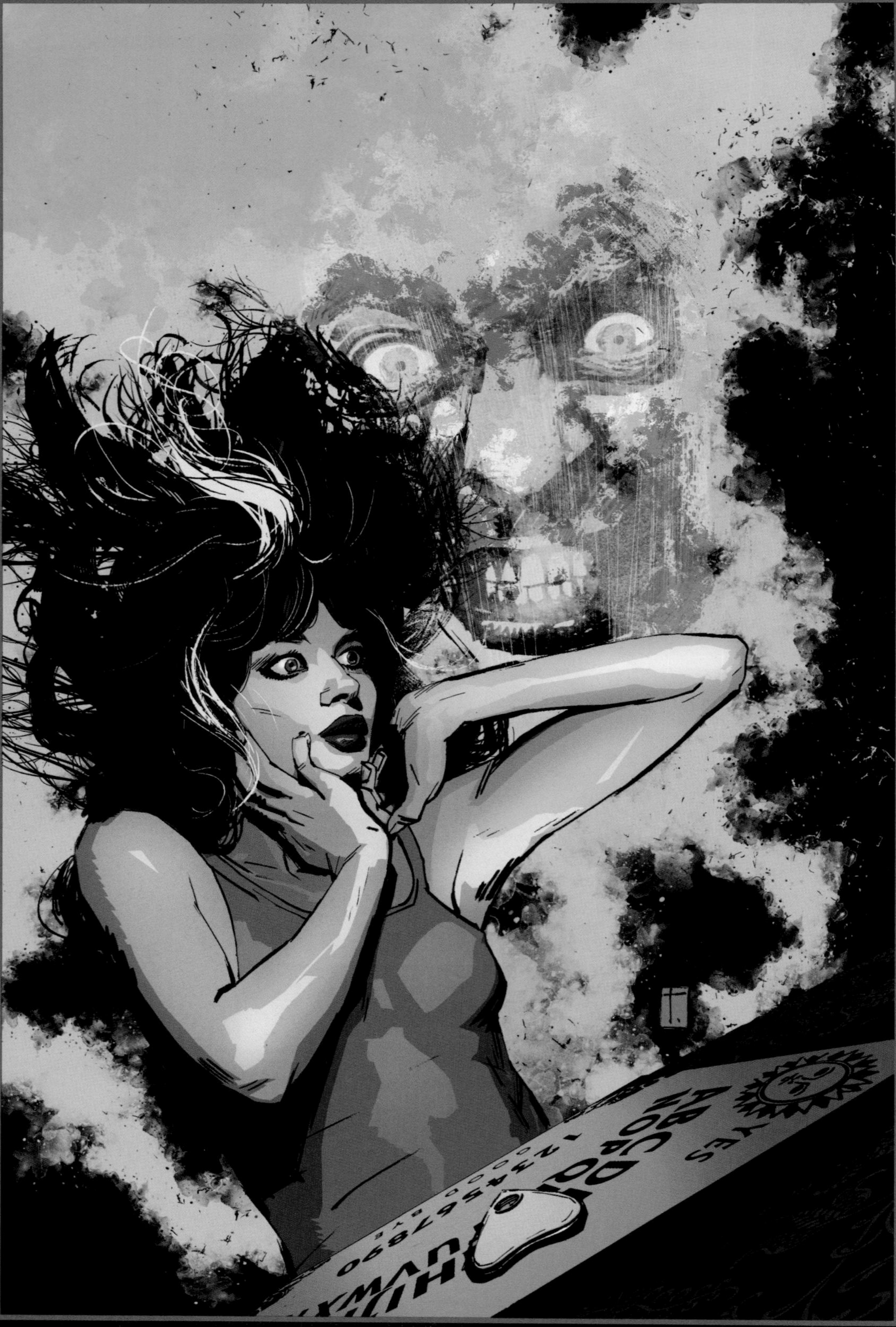
YES
1234567890

The story continues in

THE STAND:
CAPTAIN TRIPS
ISBN: 978-0-7851-4272-0

THE STAND:
AMERICAN NIGHTMARES
ISBN: 978-0-7851-4274-4

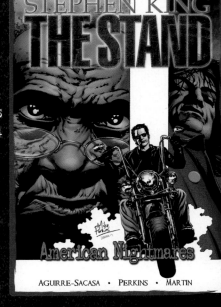

THE STAND:
SOUL SURVIVORS
ISBN: 978-0-7851-3622-4

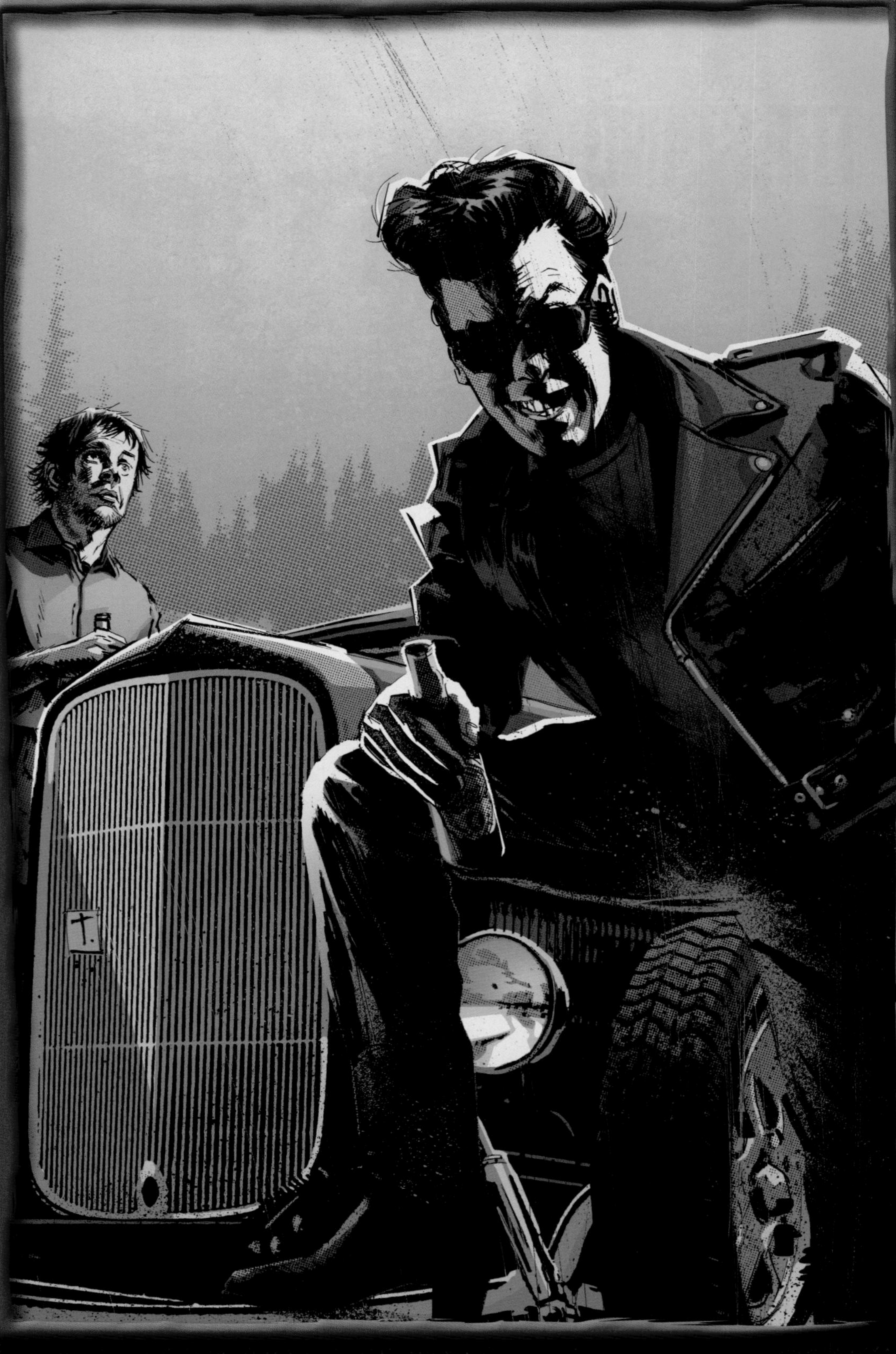

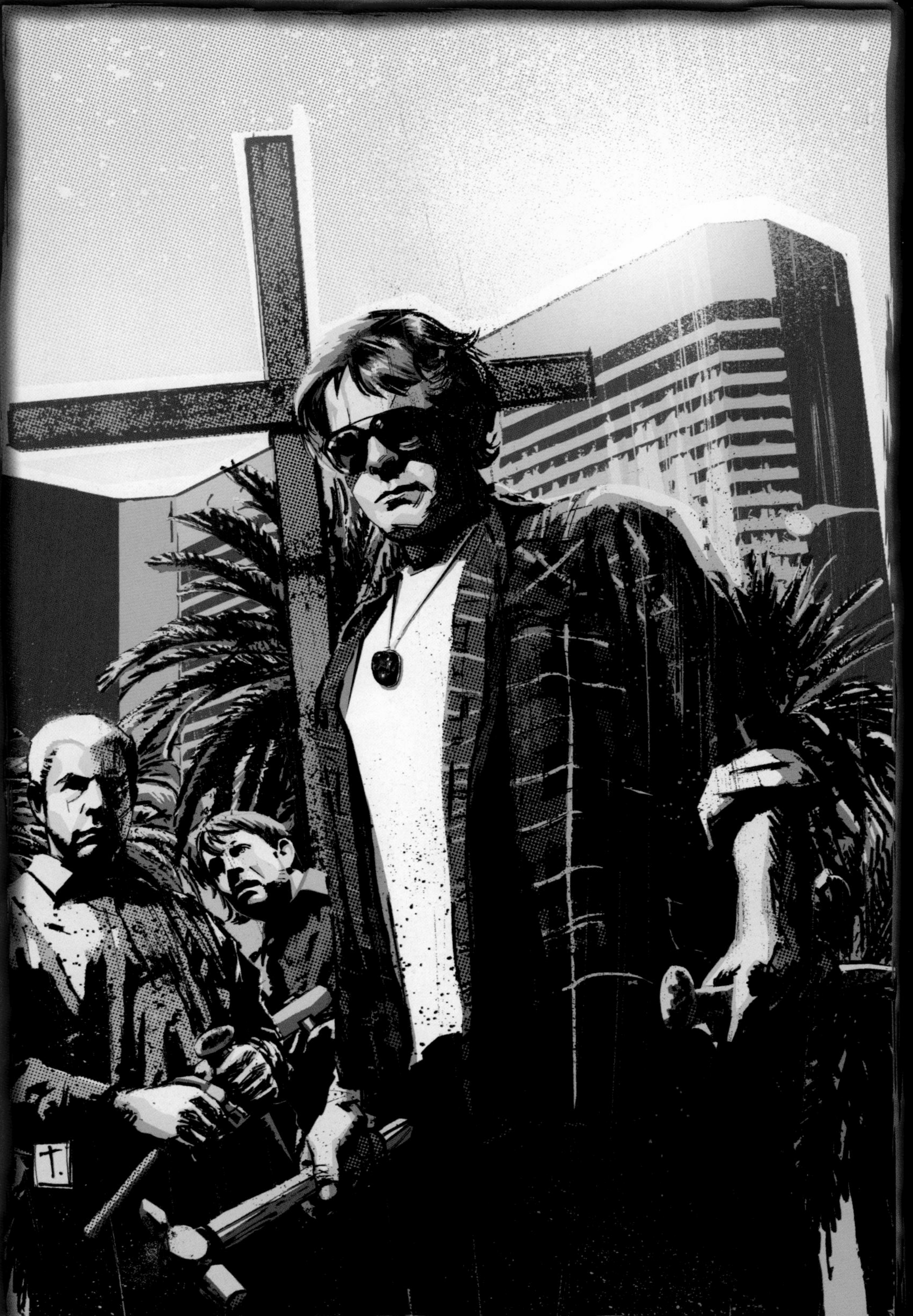

2

BOULDER
CITY LIMIT
ELEV 5345 FT
1629 M

3

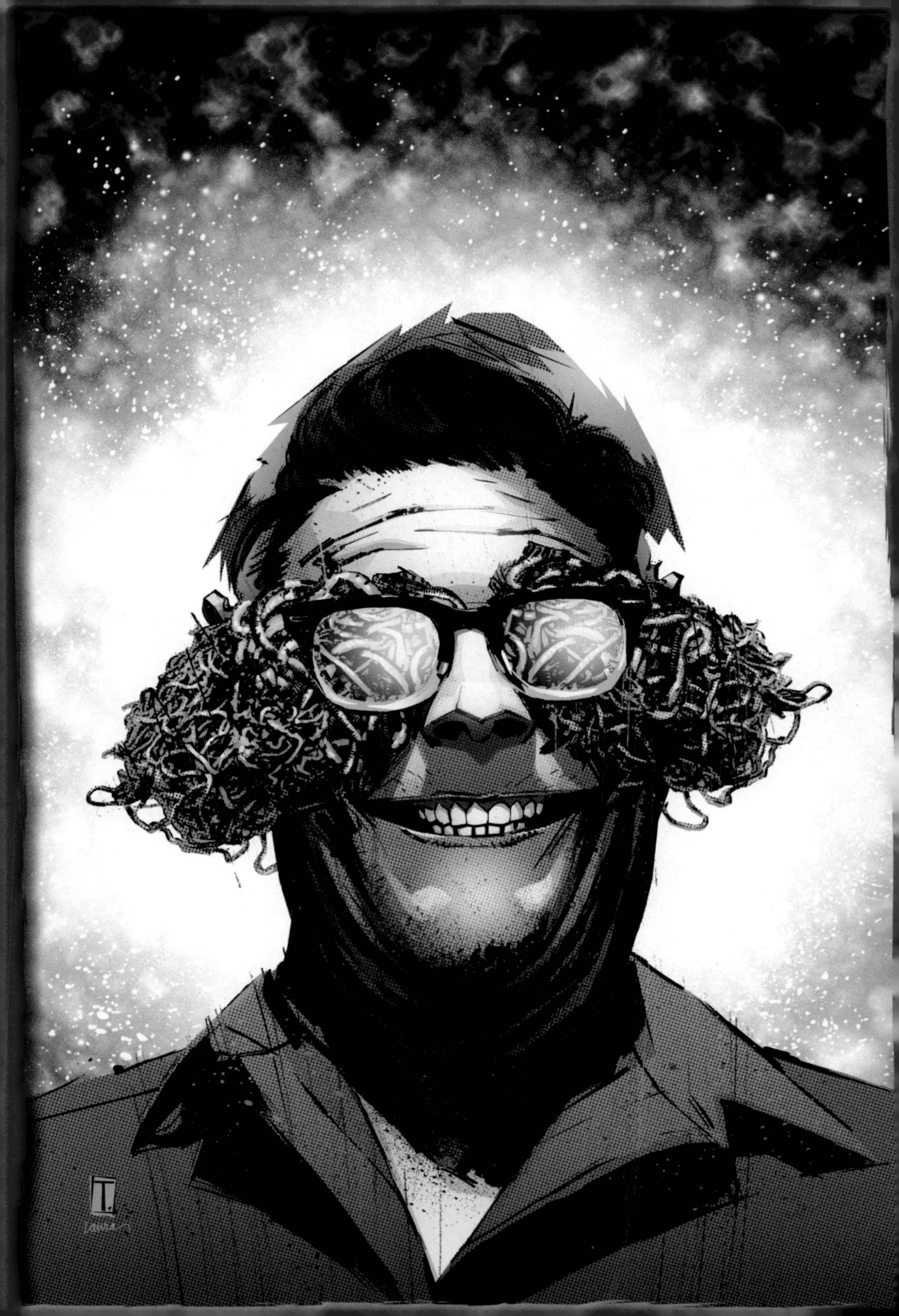

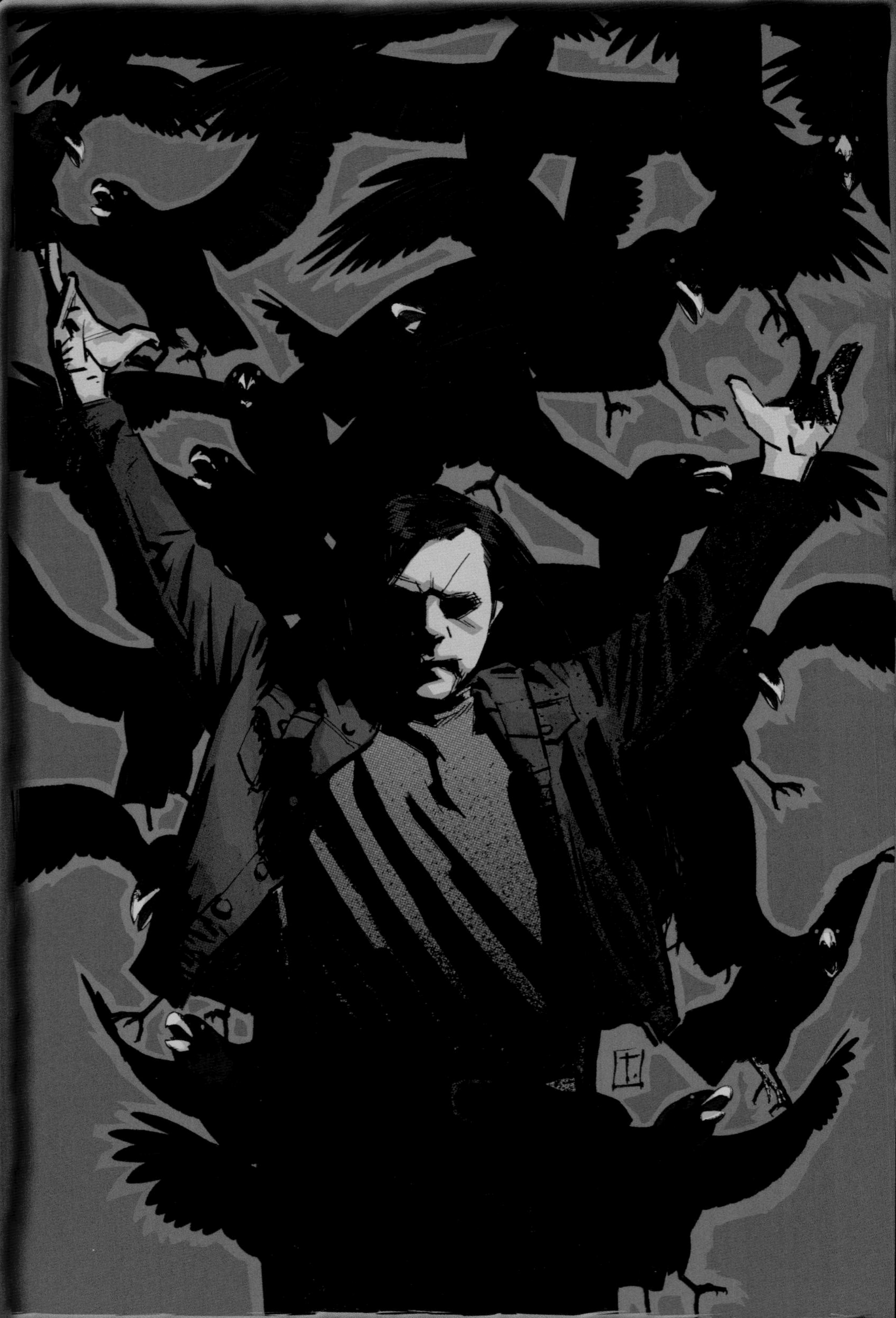

5

BOULDER DASH

Mike Perkins discusses his trip to Boulder, and drawing the city in THE STAND

I was always aware that Hardcases would be the "difficult" arc of our adaptation of Marvel's *The Stand*. From my initial read-through of the unabridged novel I could tell that when the majority of our protagonists reached Boulder they would have to endure through the growing pains of re-introducing some kind of societal norms—this usually involves a lot of chatting! I also understood that this procedure is rudimentary and importantly needed in moving things forward and establishing a reason to take... well... a Stand!

I've been extremely lucky in the respect that I've got Roberto as a fantastic collaborator. This is a guy who knows his way around drama—he understands the ins and outs of lurking tension, outright horror and character interactions, and knows when to place those elements

Here's a few comparisons from my files:

Citizens of the Free Zone inspect flyers announcing the Open Meeting in Boulder in *The Stand: Hardcases 4*.

Larry and Leo walk along a suburban street in *Hardcases 4*, en route to Harold's house.

within the narrative in order to pace the plot and accelerate the momentum.

From the offset—just as in Larry's escape from New York through the Lincoln Tunnel—I knew that the reality of the settings of this arc had to be spot on and, apart from one snafu (placing Fran and Stu in a house rather than an apartment—even though I took photos of their apartment—as seen below), I believe that's something I've been able to achieve through close observation of Boulder itself.

When I visited Boulder, Colorado, I took a multitude of photographs of the streets and homes in order to achieve some sort of authenticity to the adaptation. As I walked the neighborhoods, my mind was re-visiting the novel and ruminating about the varied and different houses corresponding to the individual characters. This is long before I'd reached the scenes in the adaptation, but some vistas pretty much drew themselves—from street scenes to vistas from Flagstaff Mountain.

From *Hardcases 3*, sunrise over the Boulder Free Zone.

Evening on one of Boulder's commercial main streets, as seen in *Hardcases 3*.

After a night of drinking, Stu and Glen discuss the future of Boulder in *Hardcases 3*.

Mother Abagail's house, as seen in *Hardcases 3*.

From *Hardcases 3*, Harold Lauder's house.

Stu and Frannie's house, seen in *Hardcases 3*, and the apartment they were supposed to live in, above right.

Stu and Larry sit on Larry's porch as Stu invites Larry to serve on the ad hoc committee in *Hardcases 4*.

travel
MAPS

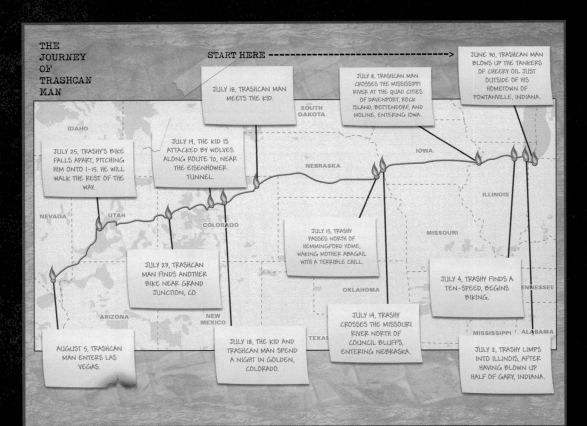

THE
JOURNEY
OF
TRASHCAN
MAN

START HERE ------------------------------>

JUNE 30, TRASHCAN MAN BLOWS UP THE TANKERS OF CHEERY OIL JUST OUTSIDE OF HIS HOMETOWN OF POWTANVILLE, INDIANA.

JULY 18, TRASHCAN MAN MEETS THE KID.

JULY 8, TRASHCAN MAN CROSSES THE MISSISSIPPI RIVER AT THE QUAD CITIES OF DAVENPORT, ROCK ISLAND, BETTENDORF, AND MOLINE, ENTERING IOWA.

JULY 25, TRASHY'S BIKE FALLS APART, PITCHING HIM ONTO I-15. HE WILL WALK THE REST OF THE WAY.

JULY 19, THE KID IS ATTACKED BY WOLVES ALONG ROUTE 70, NEAR THE EISENHOWER TUNNEL.

JULY 23, TRASHCAN MAN FINDS ANOTHER BIKE NEAR GRAND JUNCTION, CO

JULY 15, TRASHY PASSES NORTH OF HEMMINGFORD HOME, WAKING MOTHER ABAGAIL WITH A TERRIBLE CHILL.

JULY 4, TRASHY FINDS A TEN-SPEED, BEGINS BIKING.

JULY 14, TRASHY CROSSES THE MISSOURI RIVER NORTH OF COUNCIL BLUFFS, ENTERING NEBRASKA.

AUGUST 5, TRASHCAN MAN ENTERS LAS VEGAS.

JULY 18, THE KID AND TRASHCAN MAN SPEND A NIGHT IN GOLDEN, COLORADO.

JULY 2, TRASHY LIMPS INTO ILLINOIS, AFTER HAVING BLOWN UP HALF OF GARY, INDIANA.

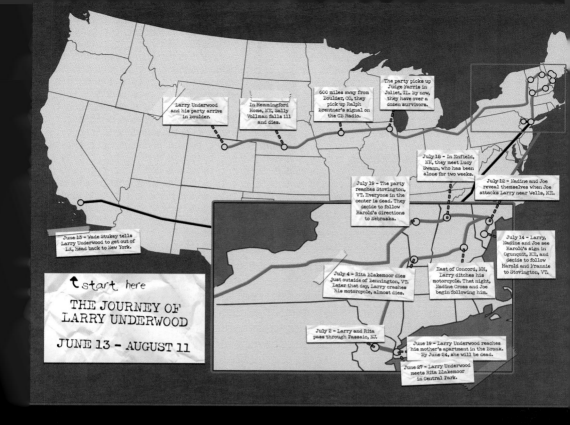

Larry Underwood and his party arrive in Boulder.

In Hemmingford Home, NE, Sally Vollman falls ill and dies.

600 miles away from Boulder, CO, they pick up Ralph Brentner's signal on the CB Radio.

The party picks up Judge Farris in Joliet, IL. By now, they have over a dozen survivors.

July 18 - In Enfield, NH, they meet Lucy Swann, who has been alone for two weeks.

July 12 - Nadine and Joe reveal themselves when Joe attacks Larry near Wells, ME.

July 19 - The party reaches Stovington, VT. Everyone in the center is dead. They decide to follow Harold's directions to Nebraska.

June 13 - Wade Stukey tells Larry Underwood to get out of LA, head back to New York.

July 14 - Larry, Nadine and Joe see Harold's sign in Ogunquit, ME, and decide to follow Harold and Frannie to Stovington, VT.

July 4 - Rita Blakemoor dies just outside of Bennington, VT. Later that day, Larry crashes his motorcycle, almost dies.

East of Concord, NH, Larry ditches his motorcycle. That night, Nadine Cross and Joe begin following him.

↰ start here

THE JOURNEY OF LARRY UNDERWOOD

JUNE 13 - AUGUST 11

July 2 - Larry and Rita pass through Passaic, NJ.

June 19 - Larry Underwood reaches his mother's apartment in the Bronx. By June 24, she will be dead.

June 27 - Larry Underwood meets Rita Blakemoor in Central Park.

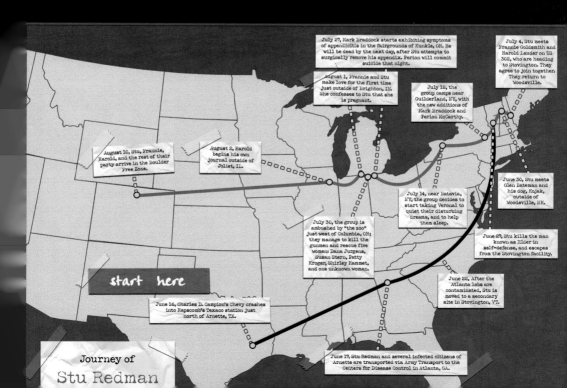

July 27, Mark Braddock starts exhibiting symptoms of appendicitis in the fairgrounds of Kunkle, OH. He will be dead by the next day, after Stu attempts to surgically remove his appendix. Perion will commit suicide that night.

July 4, Stu meets Frannie Goldsmith and Harold Lauder on US 302, who are heading to Stovington. They agree to join together. They return to Woodsville.

August 1, Frannie and Stu make love for the first time just outside of Brighton, IN. She confesses to Stu that she is pregnant.

July 12, the group camps near Guilderland, NY, with the new additions of Mark Braddock and Perion McCarthy.

August 10, Stu, Frannie, Harold, and the rest of their party arrive in the Boulder Free Zone.

August 2, Harold begins his own journal outside of Joliet, IL.

July 14, near Batavia, NY, the group decides to start taking Veronal to quiet their disturbing dreams, and to help them sleep.

June 30, Stu meets Glen Bateman and his dog, Kojak, outside of Woodsville, NH.

July 30, the group is ambushed by "the zoo" just west of Columbia, OH; they manage to kill the gunmen and rescue five women; Dana Jurgens, Susan Stern, Patty Kroger, Shirley Hammet, and one unknown woman.

June 27, Stu kills the man known as Elder in self-defense, and escapes from the Stovington facility.

start here

June 22, After the Atlanta labs are contaminated, Stu is moved to a secondary site in Stovington, VT.

June 16, Charles D. Campion's Chevy crashes into Hapscomb's Texaco station just north of Arnette, TX.

Journey of
Stu Redman

June 17, Stu Redman and several infected citizens of Arnette are transported via Army Transport to the Centers for Disease Control in Atlanta, GA.

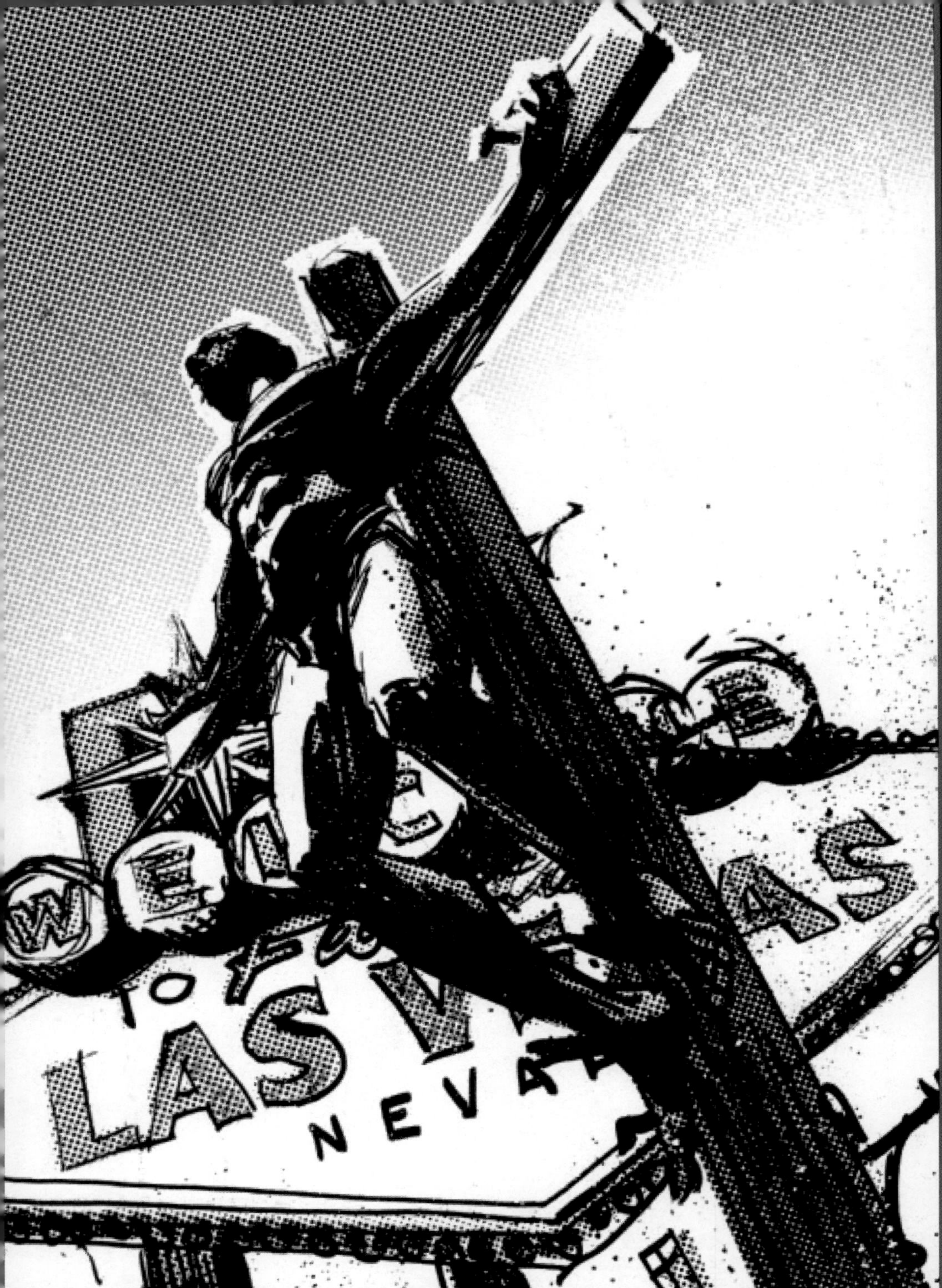
TO
LAS
NEVA